THE BLESSINGS OF
IMPERFECTION

The
Blessings of
Imperfection
Reflections
on the
Mystery of
Everyday
Life
G. Peter
Fleck

Beacon Press • Boston

Beacon Press
25 Beacon Street
Boston, Massachusetts 02108-2892
www.beacon.org

Beacon Press books
are published under the auspices of
the Unitarian Universalist Association of Congregations.

First digital-print edition 2001

Library of Congress Cataloging-in-Publication Data
Fleck, G. Peter.
The blessings of imperfection.
ISBN 0-8070-1605-5
1. Spiritual life—Unitarian Universalist authors. I. Title.
BL624.F55   1987
248.4   87-47538

To Ann, Andrea, and Marjorie
and to the memory of Jan Melchior

Contents

Foreword

In March 1941, Peter and Ruth Fleck were able to leave their native Holland, after having lived for ten months under Nazi occupation. Shortly after arriving in the United States, Peter discovered Unitarianism. It was love at first sight. For more than four decades he has played an active role in the Unitarian Universalist denomination, serving on numerous denominational boards and committees, taking a vigorous interest in the professional theological education of ministers, and making himself a name as a lay preacher. In 1984, ten years after retiring from a distinguished banking career, Peter was ordained as a Unitarian Universalist minister, becoming minister associate of First Parish Brewster, Brewster, Massachusetts.

Relatively little reference to the Holocaust appears in the present volume, though occasionally the author draws back the curtain "on our cruel age" in which "many have met death in concentration camps, on battlefields, in the slums of the third world's overcrowded, swollen cities. . . ." Nor are there here any references to his Wall Street career.

What is striking is the range of human problems "unpacked" in a remarkably lively, down-to-earth, and engaging style, with insights and illustrations drawn from Scripture and poetry and other literature, from the rabbinic as well as the ecumenical Christian tradition. Here we find a treasure trove assembled over a period of more than seven decades. Seldom does one find here anything like conventional piety; rather, one encounters a unique individual ruminating on the problems of our everyday existence. I am tempted here to use the phrase from Phillips Brooks—"truth reflected through personality."

This book is a lucid, imaginative introduction to perennial problems of ethics and theology—set forth with modesty and a dash of skepticism.

The title essay of course gives the basic motif of a major theme of the volume, that failure is a part of imperfect humanity, and indeed may also open a path toward perfection. On reading this chapter I was immediately reminded of the story of Leonardo da Vinci: One morning he went to look at his new painting *The Madonna of the Rocks,* which was on exhibition. He overheard other viewers speaking with superlative praise of the picture, but he was far from satisfied with it. He turned away, saying to himself, "They do not even understand what I was trying to do."

The recognition of imperfection itself bespeaks two things. First it may serve as a protection against demonic pretensions, especially against demonic religious pretensions. Second, it points beyond to a divine resource of power and judgment. If a rock casts a shadow, then there is a sun behind. Of this shadow, Dr. Fleck asserts, we should never be silent, lest we sink into darkness—John Milton here used the phrase "darkness visible."

The tenor of this book is serene and genial. But its burden is to call for a critical understanding and renewal of faith. It calls for a sense of community in the midst of our frustrations and imperfections.

James Luther Adams

Acknowledgments

I am grateful to Wendy Strothman, Director of Beacon Press, for the enthusiasm with which she accepted this book for publication, and to Thomas Fischer, Managing Editor of Beacon Press, for the great expertise with which he helped me make my essays into a book. I thank Pam Pokorney, Beacon's Production Manager, who so ably oversaw the design and production of the book, and Margaret Gilmore for her great competence and dedication in typing the manuscript.

A special word of thanks to Jeannette Hopkins, who gave me the benefit of her guidance in the process of converting sermon material into essays.

Above all I thank my dear wife Ruth for her creative support, her patient friendship, and her love.

G. Peter Fleck

1

Being
Imperfect

1

The Blessings of Imperfection

*And Moses went up from the plains of Moab
unto the mountain of Nebo. . . . And the Lord
said unto him, This is the land which I sware
unto Abraham, unto Isaac, and unto Jacob,
saying, I will give it unto thy seed: I have
caused thee to see it with thine eyes, but thou
shalt not go over thither.*

Deuteronomy 34:1, 4

*We have evolved scientists . . . and so we
know a lot about DNA, but if our kind of mind
had been confronted with the problem of de-
signing a similar replicating molecule . . .
we'd never have succeeded. We would have
made one fatal mistake: our molecule would
have been perfect. . . . The capacity to blunder
slightly is the real marvel of DNA. Without
this special attribute we would still be anaer-
obic bacteria and there would be no music.*

Lewis Thomas
The Medusa and the Snail

I want to tell you a story my mother used to read to
me before I could read for myself. The story—I
think it was Scandinavian—fascinated me and I
asked her to read it to me again and again, as
children will.

4

It was the story of a gnome who lived in the forest under the root of a tree. He had one big wish: more than anything else in the world he wanted to own a green hunter's bag. He used to think about his green hunter's bag by day and to dream about it at night. He had visualized it a thousand times. Then, one day, it may have been his birthday, he received a beautiful green hunter's bag as a gift. His dream had come true; his ardent wish had been fulfilled. He owned his green hunter's bag. Now you would have expected him to be happy. But he said, "It is a nice hunter's bag, only it is not quite as green as I had imagined it."

Some seventy years have passed and I still recall the impression that story made on me, the feelings it elicited. They were the feelings of a child who is initiated into one of the secrets of the adult world. For the story describes a situation to which none of us are strangers. All of us, at times, have experienced the sadness of disappointment upon the fulfillment of an ardent wish. The stream was not quite as clear as we had imagined it; the sea not quite as blue; the mountains not quite as overpowering; the woods not quite as dark; our marriage not quite as happy; our children not quite as accomplished. Reality did not measure up to our idea of reality. And when we say that, we have stated one of the principal tenets of the philosophy of Plato. For Plato taught that only the idea of something is perfect and its realization, its expression in material, worldly terms, a mere shadow of that perfection.

I believe that something similar to this Platonic thought may be imputed to the story of creation as told in the book of Genesis. During the week-long process of creation, when God inspects the results of his daily endeavors, he pronounces them "good"—not "perfect," mind you, just "good." "Good" in this text, according to the 1919 edition of Peake's *Commentary on the Bible,* means "entirely adequate to its purpose," for it "was precisely what He had intended."[1] But adequate for what purpose, and what did God intend? Obviously these are no longer realistic questions. Still, I will try to formulate a realistic answer to them. One could say that the imperfection of creation is meant to challenge humankind to make creation less imperfect, and that creation has endowed humankind with the means to do just that. And so it is that imperfect men and women are engaged in the process of trying to make an imperfect world more perfect. The words of the hymn come to mind:

> *Creation's Lord we give thee thanks*
> *That this thy world is incomplete . . .*
> *That we are in the making still. . . .*

What if the world were ever complete? There would be nothing left to be done; the human task would be fulfilled, the human role ended.

Don't worry. While we may—yes, must—strive for perfection, perfection is not attainable. It is the striving toward perfection that counts. Only the idea of something can be perfect. Its material expression, or, to use a loaded word, its incarnation, cannot be perfect. The actual hunter's bag is never as perfectly green as the idea of it. But the memory of the idea's perfection lingers on, and makes us seek to regain that perfection.

It is in this light that I interpret the incident in Moses' life that led to the Lord's denying him the right to enter the promised land. That incident has always puzzled me. There was Moses, laboring day after day, year after year, first to get his people out of Egypt, then to lead them on their long pilgrimage through the desert to the promised land, acting all the time as an intermediary, a buffer between a difficult God and a difficult people, fulfilling a job for which he had not volunteered—unselfishly, devotedly, religiously. And then he slips once, just once, for even Moses is not perfect. And it was not even such a bad slip: just for once he forgot to say that the power that enabled him to get water out of the rock was not his power but the Lord's. And—bingo—he is punished with an apparently cruel punishment: he will not be allowed to enter the promised land; it will be shown to him from a distance but he will not be among the children of Israel when they enter the land promised to their fathers.

To me it had always appeared that the Lord inflicted an unduly severe punishment upon his exemplary servant, until, one day recently, it dawned upon me that—maybe—what appeared a cruel punishment was in reality a gracious blessing in disguise. For the Lord gave Moses a view of the promised land from afar: how beautiful the hills, how mysterious the forests, how clear the water, how green the valleys, how incredibly green. It was perfect—as perfect as only the idea, the vision, of something can be. Moses was blessed for the Lord saved him from witnessing the realization of that vision which was to be but a shadow of the beauty he had seen. Then he died "according to the word of the Lord," as the Bible says, transfixed by the beauty of his vision. "And he," the Lord, "buried him . . ." (Deuteronomy 34:5–6).

In his book *The Medusa and the Snail*, the biologist Lewis Thomas observes that we humans "are built to make mistakes, coded for error," that is, for being imperfect. "We learn, as we say, by trial and error. . . . Why not 'trial and rightness' or 'trial and triumph?' " And he concludes: "The old phrase puts it that way because that is, in real life, the way it is done."[2] In other words: progress requires error. What persuasive reasoning: our response to our imperfection, he seems to say, is the very thing that can make us more perfect. Indeed: "The capacity to leap across mountains of information to land lightly on the wrong side represents the highest of human endowments."[3] Assuming, of course, that you do something about having landed on the wrong side.

This principle does not apply to humans only. It permeates creation. It is the very stuff of which evolution is made. Take the amphibians. The first one that crawled out of the water onto the land may not have done so because its feet were so strong, but because its gills were so weak. The imperfection of its gills made that first amphibian into an animal of a higher order. But one can imagine its parents' distress at having a child that was so conspicuously unable to live a normal aquatic life, a child with which there was obviously something wrong, and one can imagine how it was jeered at by its peers. Nor did that first amphibian have any idea of what was happening to it. It had no idea that its "wrongness" had led it into a "betterness."

Humans are the only creatures on this earth to whom it is given to be aware of the wrongness, the error, the imperfection in themselves and to react to that wrongness in a way that tends to overcome it. And if it cannot be overcome, to accept it as inevitable and to live with it. The resolve to make one's peace and live with inevitable imperfection is a creative act.

Take the case of organized religion. All of us have friends or acquaintances who maintain that they are not irreligious but who refuse to become members of a church because, they say, they cannot stand organized religion. "I believe in God," one of them once said to me, "I pray in the privacy of my home, I try to live a decent life, I give money to charities, but I do not want to have anything to do with organized religion."

Well, let's be frank and admit that the church has its aggravations. The eternal and oh-so-necessary concern about finances, the annually recurring problems of balancing a budget, of finding money for repainting the vestibule, repairing the boiler, and tuning the organ, the ongoing criticism of the minister's sermons, which are too liberal for some and too orthodox for others, too pedantic for some and too colloquial for others, the endless committee meetings about the Sunday school curriculum and about the propriety of social action, the persistent shortage of tenors in the choir. Who wants it? Who needs it?

The answer to this question is that *we*, all of us, the congregation and the minister, want it, because we need it. The answer is that the church, and I am now speaking of the liberal church, in spite of its shortcomings, the imperfection that characterizes everything made by humans, is better, infinitely better, than no church. Maybe I should not have said "in spite of its shortcomings" but "because of its shortcomings." For isn't it true that in our churches, in these communities of the spirit, we have more resources than outside of our churches to accept each other's imperfections, to reconcile our differences, to forgive and be forgiven, to comfort and to be comforted, to love and to be loved? Isn't that what the church is all about— because that is what life is all about? There is no contradiction between trying to overcome imperfection, to strive for, hope for, perfection, while at the same time accepting the fact that perfection is not in the cards. Human institutions will be imperfect because men and women are imperfect. But that is no reason for abolishing these institutions without which there is no civilization. We have to be tolerant of their imperfection while striving for perfection. We have to recognize that it is imperfection that gives meaning to the human enterprise. In that sense imperfection is a blessing.

The same applies to us. You are imperfect. I am imperfect, all of us are. To say "You're OK, I'm OK" is mere whistling in the dark. But that is no reason to do away with ourselves, though it may be a reason to feel humble in our efforts to overcome our imperfections while acknowledging, at the same time, that perfection is not of this world.

The only time the world was perfect was before it was created. When it was still but an idea, a glint in the creator's eye. But when it was put together in matter, when it materialized, it was no longer perfect; it was good. It was as good as possible.

2

Be Not Angry with Yourself

> I am Joseph your brother, whom ye sold into
> Egypt. Now therefore be not grieved, nor
> angry with yourselves, that ye sold me hither:
> for God did send me before you to preserve life.
>
> Genesis 45:4–5

> Sin not; let not the sun go down upon your
> wrath.
>
> Ephesians 4:26

Are you ever angry with yourself? I mean really angry, mad? I know I am. And I have a hunch that many of you are; maybe most of you; possibly all. At times. And, frequently, for no good reason. Take the other day: I was to attend a meeting at ten o'clock in Wellfleet, half an hour's drive from our house. That morning all kinds of things happened so that I was still at home at five minutes of ten. I hate being late for meetings and was furious at myself for having neglected to keep track of the time. I got there at twenty past ten to find that I was the first to arrive. The meeting had been set, not for ten o'clock, but for ten-thirty! Then I became angry with myself for having been angry with myself for the wrong reason, and then my anger vanished, for after all I did get there in time. But even if I had been late, I am sure that my anger would not have lasted beyond my arrival; for basically there was nothing to be angry about.

When I come to think of it, I am really angry with myself several times a day: someone has called who had just lost her mother; I should have been warmer in expressing my condolences. I owed somebody an answer about a speaking engagement; it was overdue and my negligence would no doubt be interpreted as a lack of enthusiasm—which it was—and hurt my host's feelings. An acquaintance of ours was blessed with the birth of twins and I sent "best wishes for mother and child."

Anger with oneself does not necessarily involve another person. I can be mad at myself for having missed an opportunity, for having done something that prejudices my future, for having spoken when it would have been better to keep quiet, or for having kept quiet when I should have spoken up. I may be angry with myself because, in the words of the apostle Paul: "The good that I would I do not; but the evil which I would not that I do."

Having a bad conscience is not the same as being angry at oneself. A bad conscience comes from having committed an ethically or morally objectionable act that causes suffering to another or to others. It always involves another person, even if the act is hidden from the world and committed in secret.

A bad conscience can be relieved by sharing the secret with someone else, that is, by confessing it. The Catholic church, through the process of confession, imposition of penance, and absolution can relieve the believer's conscience. In a similar way others may confess to their therapist. Unlike the priest, the therapist is not judgmental and there is no question of penalties; only of understanding the motives of what one did.

The Lutherans hold that forgiveness can be gained by faith: don't indulge in a bad conscience; have faith in God's infinite goodness and power and you will be forgiven. Most liberal religionists do not share this belief. The liberal conscience is relieved not by faith but by works. You will be forgiven not because of your faith but because of your way of life.

I would submit that the ultimate relief from a bad conscience comes from being forgiven not by God but by the victim of the bad-conscience-causing deed. In fact, there is a tradition in Judaism which holds that even God cannot forgive the culprit, only the victim can.

Two personal tragedies experienced by two of Jesus' disciples illustrate the point. Peter denied him thrice. Then the cock crowed and he went out and wept bitterly. Tears of anger at himself. Judas betrayed Jesus. Then he tried to undo what he had done by returning the thirty silver pieces. But those who had tempted him laughed at him. It was too late. "And he cast down the pieces of silver in the temple, and departed and hanged himself." His betrayal of "the innocent blood," as Matthew puts it, was more than his conscience could bear. Only one person could have forgiven him: the victim, Jesus. But he was no longer accessible. Poor Judas. For I have always believed that Jesus would have forgiven him, if only because without the act of betrayal there would have been no salvation. At least not according to good, orthodox Christian doctrine.

Peter's threefold denial on the other hand victimized nobody but himself. He was the only one who could forgive himself. And he did.

The word *angry* derives from the Latin *angor*, meaning *anguish*, all three from the root *ang*, which we find in the Latin verb *ango*, that is, to press tight, to throttle; in the German word *Angst*, that is, fear; and in the Dutch word *eng*, which means both *narrow* and *eerie, uncanny*. So the word *angry* contains elements of fear, uncanniness, narrowness. It is claustrophobic, there is no exit, no way out. That is why anger is explosive and often seems uncontrollable. And still we must control that anger, whether it is aimed at ourselves or at somebody else. Often the two are intermingled.

I think they were intermingled for Joseph's brothers when Joseph made himself known to them. They were angry at Joseph: in their early years he had dreamed of being superior to his brothers, of commanding their obedience. And now he had achieved it. He had played a cat-and-mouse game with them, testing their love for their youngest brother Benjamin, and in retrospect they were angry with him. But they were also angry with themselves for having lent themselves to Joseph's manipulations, for not having been as smart as their younger brother, for needing him now and for being in his power. And their anger with themselves—as it does so often—incapacitated them: "And Joseph said unto his brethren, I am Joseph; doth my father yet live? And his brethren could not answer him; for they were troubled at his presence." Then Joseph showed his real superiority by the manner in which he assuaged their anger:

> And Joseph said unto his brethren . . .
> Come near to me, I pray you. And they
> came near. And he said, I am Joseph your
> brother whom ye sold into Egypt. Now

therefore be not grieved, nor angry with
yourselves, that ye sold me hither: for God
did send me before you to preserve life . . .
to preserve you a posterity in the earth, and
to save your lives by a great deliverance.
(Genesis 45:3–7)

He made it easier for them to forgive themselves,
to give up their anger by placing their anger-
provoking act within the scope of God's plan. He
made them feel that they had been God's co-
workers in providing the means of their rescue
from the famine in their own country by having
sold their younger brother into Egypt many, many
years ago. And as soon as they had forgiven
themselves, they recovered the energy to function,
to respond, to react: "And he kissed all his brothers and wept on them, and after that his brothers
talked with him." For anger at oneself consumes
energy, and freedom from anger releases it.

John McEnroe, the tennis champion with the
vile—and, at times, I find, ingratiating—temper,
said after winning the men's singles at Wimbledon:

I purposely remained calm and preserved
my energy for the match. I wasted a lot of
energy in Paris [where he had barely won a
tournament a few weeks earlier] getting
angry at myself.[1]

On June 20, 1984, President Reagan visited a
high school in Oradel, New Jersey, that apparently
had developed a highly successful program to
combat drunken driving. The president seemed
impressed and touched by the testimony of nine-
teen-year-old Hector Del Valle, who had been a
champion gymnast before, what he called, "one

stupid night," when he was drunk and drove his car into a brick wall, paralyzing himself for life. "The tough-guy bit is an act, and if you are smart you'll drop it," Hector Del Valle told the crowd of youngsters. Still, he had come far in rehabilitating himself. "Just think, I can't move my fingers, but here I am getting ready to shake the hand of the President of the United States." His final words to the young people were a touching "Take care."[2] Hector Del Valle had overcome what must have been deep anger at himself, anger for paralyzing himself for no good reason. He had no Joseph to help him overcome it. Perhaps his parents, his friends, his siblings, his minister or priest helped him. We don't know. But he did overcome it. And in overcoming his anger with himself, he demonstrated how creative the act of forgiving oneself can be, how it frees energies, how it recreates one's responsiveness to others.

Being angry with oneself is a barren preoccupation. It wages a losing battle with the past. For what is done is done. One has to live with it, even if it is embarrassing, hurtful, imperfect. Ah, that's the word: imperfect. Because, in the last analysis, our anger at ourselves is aimed at our imperfection. We want to be perfect, we want to do and say the right things, to stand for the right things. Toward everybody, parents, children, friends. Forget it. Reality just isn't structured that way. Our imperfection is God-given. We have to live with our imperfection. In humility.

In saying this, do I advocate stoicism? I don't think so. I don't say: accept your imperfections, period. Rather: do something about them, or at least try to do something about them, by all means. But do not stay angry with yourself if the result falls short of perfection.

In the sermon on the mount, Jesus said:

If thou bring thy gift to the altar, and there
rememberest that thy brother hath aught
against thee; leave thy gift before the altar
and go thy way; first be reconciled to thy
brother, and then come and offer thy gift.
(Matthew 5:23–24)

I believe that the same applies to ourselves.

First be reconciled to thyself, and then come and
offer thy gift.

3

The Messiness of It All

Those masterful images because complete
Grew in pure mind, but out of what began?
A mound of refuse or the sweepings of a street,
Old kettles, old bottles, and a broken can,
Old iron, old bones, old rags, that raving slut
Who keeps the till. Now that my ladder's gone,
I must lie down where all the ladders start,
In the foul rag-and-bone shop of the heart.

William Butler Yeats
"The Circus Animals' Desertion"

I have nothing to offer but blood, toil, tears
and sweat.

Winston Churchill
First Statement as Prime Minister,
House of Commons, May 3, 1940

You who have given birth to children and you who have witnessed this most exhilarating of all human experiences, when life brings forth life, you know that giving birth is a messy business. For we are born in blood and gore. Creativity is marked by messiness. It takes a degree of resignation to accept this disillusioning insight. Maybe a degree of wisdom. The very young have neither.

I am reminded of the story of Benjamin. Benjamin is a grandson of ours. He was born and spent his early years in a small university town in Iowa, surrounded by farms. At the age of four, reflecting his environment, he owned an imaginary farm. From time to time he told his parents what was going on there. One day he said to his mother: "Mom, you know what happened last night? Last night the vet came and you know what he did? He cut a little piece off the hoof of the cow and now she has a calf." His mother, who has a talent for seizing opportunities when they present themselves, felt that this was the moment to introduce her four-year-old son to the facts of life. "Benjamin," she said, "this is not the way it happens." And then she embarked on a long story about sperm and fertilization and how the embryo develops in the womb and how the little calf is finally born between the cow's legs. "You see, Benjamin," she said, "that is how it really happens." Whereupon Benjamin looked her straight in the eye and said: "Not on *my* farm."

You see, Benjamin was not ready to accept the ambiguity of life's messiness. He still lived in the world of fantasies and fairy tales in which things happen without effort, just like that. But we know that in the real world it isn't that way at all, that in the real world nothing happens without the proverbial blood, sweat, and tears and that the birth of a calf or a child or a symphony or a theology is invariably attended by at least one of these three. This can be very grievous.

A few months ago we saw and heard on television the Vienna Philharmonic Orchestra perform Beethoven's Seventh Symphony, under the direction of Leonard Bernstein. Bernstein, as he is wont to do, introduced the performance. He stressed that when the master wrote this symphony he had already lost most of his hearing. In fact, according to his biographer Schauffler,[1] Beethoven began to lose his hearing at the age of twenty-eight and the horror of his oncoming deafness may account, at least in part, for his irritability, his eccentricity, the instability of his relationships with those he loved one day and hated the next. In part, I say, for the tremendous creativity that made him sing, pound the piano, write music by day and by night would not, in any case, have permitted him to find the domestic peace, the tranquility, and the happiness he craved. The passion with which he tried, after the death of his brother, to play father to his brother's nine-year-old son Karl led to one disaster after the other, including Karl's unsuccessful suicide attempt. Beethoven neglected himself, walked around unkempt and in old clothes. He was sick much of the time, distracted by hopeless domestic affairs, aggravated by the morbid suspicion that haunts some of the deaf. Bernstein closed his short remarks of introduction with the words: "And in this torturous frame sang the voice of an angel."

Speaking of angels: it has been said that when the souls of the dead enter heaven, the angels play music by Bach, but that when among themselves they play Mozart. However, the young Mozart, as correctly portrayed in Peter Schafer's play *Amadeus*, was a vulgar little guy who loved to use four-letter words and to behave accordingly. So, once again we are confronted with the incredible combination of divine creativity and messiness.

In 1973 an uproar was caused in intellectual and theological circles by the publication of a book that dealt with the messiness in the life of one of the great and most widely respected thinkers and theologians of the century, Paul Tillich. The book, written by his widow Hannah Tillich, revealed sordid details of their married life and of his personal predilections. So we learn from Mrs. Tillich that her husband, whom she and their close friends called "Paulus," at times would "throw a desperate temper tantrum" and that he had an inclination to pornography. "He would cover a pornographic book with an acceptable book during his rest hour," wrote Hannah Tillich, "of course his many ladyfriends took pleasure in it. To them it was a welcome basis for conversation."[2] About her wedding to Paulus, she wrote: "When our mutual divorces came through we were married. . . . On our trip home Paulus told me that he planned to go out that same evening . . . [a friend] had arranged a final bachelor's outing for him and I was not invited. I was stunned and infuriated . . . Paulus insisted that nothing untoward would take place and he left."[3]

The book caused a furor in the theological world and consternation among Tillich's friends and admirers. Some felt deeply shocked by his wife's indiscreet disclosures; others refused to give the book any credence. The thought that a man of Tillich's stature, of Tillich's spiritual genius, could have had such a messy private life was unacceptable to them. Of course, things like that happened to other people but—to paraphrase Benjamin—"not on Tillich's farm."

The fact of the matter, however, is that spirituality and creativity and genius do not exclude messiness and, at times, thrive on it. That is why I say to you be suspicious of the *absence* of messiness. What is a permissible illusion at the age of four becomes an impermissible delusion at the age of forty. Beware of the fallacy that the good and the beautiful go together and exclude messiness, for that is not so. True, the ancient Greek's ideal was the human being who was both *kalos*, beautiful, and *agathos*, virtuous. But our Judeo-Christian tradition, which was born in the blood and gore of

Jewish history and of the Crucifixion, is skeptical about the combination of virtue and beauty. The Greeks could, with impunity, deny that messiness is indispensable. But that was when Western civilization was still young, when, culturally speaking, it was in the Benjamin stage. But when this ideal is presented to us in our day and age, there is every reason to be skeptical. One might go a step further and say: Beware of the absence of messiness because it may indicate that you are no longer dealing with reality but are acting out a fantasy. The Nazi nightmare was such a fantasy. Its ideal was the blond, blue-eyed Nazi youth whose racial purity—whatever that may have meant—was supposed to guarantee the virtue of his actions and to save the world. Its pagan liturgy was the mass demonstration in which hundreds of thousands were manipulated into perfectly staged manifestations of tribute to the man-god Hitler. There was blood and gore, but it was confined to those who in that crazy fantasy were condemned to play the part of the victims. It did not touch the victimizers. In fact, it enhanced the credibility of their fantasy just as in the medieval mind the credibility of the eternal bliss of the saved in heaven was enhanced by the miserable fate of the condemned in hell.

Our lives are full of messiness. That means we are in touch with reality. In an essay on preaching, the Unitarian Universalist minister Roy D. Phillips, speaking of what he calls "the sacramental element in preaching," says:

> I know about the paper and the typewriter
> or . . . the pencil—the work of preparation.
> I know about the starting and the stopping,
> the sweating, the crossing out and the
> erasing. I know about the interruptions to

check a thesaurus or a dictionary, the
searching and the waiting for the coming of
the right word. . . .
The crossed-out, caret-marked essay
carried into the pulpit by a sweaty-palmed
human being concerned about projecting the
voice and emphasizing the proper words
. . . so very much of *this* world—incomplete
in knowledge, not ever as prepared as we
might have been for this particular Sunday's
venture . . . this human person with a
tattered essay to share . . . precisely *this* is
the sacramental element.[4]

These few sentences illustrate the messiness of the
business of writing sermons, the delivery of which
may at times amount to a sacramental act. Messiness is often a corollary of creativity.

We should be grateful for this. Even if it takes
the form of difficulties in our marriage or crises in
our relationships with our children or disappointments in our career, lost opportunities, wasted
time, broken friendships, lost tempers. For it is in
dealing with the messiness in our life that we
celebrate its creativity and its holiness.

Now that my ladder's gone,
I must lie down where all the ladders start,
In the foul rag-and-bone shop of the heart.[5]

A middle-aged woman, one of many children of
another famous theologian, once told me about her
feelings for the exemplary man who was her father. She experienced his superiority, his self-
control, his even-temperedness as coldness.
"When one of the children had misbehaved," she
told me, "he would after dinner ask the transgres-
sor to come to his study, lecture him or her on the

sin that had been committed and then dismiss the
sinner with a kiss on the forehead. Oh, how I
hated those kisses," she said. "Once I woke up in
the middle of the night to hear a lot of noise. My
older brother had come home drunk and my father
was furious. For once his self-control was gone. He
screamed at my brother. At that moment I loved
my father."

She loved him not for his strength but for his
weakness; she loved him because for once he was
not superior but just human. It must have been a
vulgar and messy scene, that father yelling at his
son in the middle of the night. But it was this scene
that redeemed the father in the eyes of his daughter. It was this messiness that enabled her to love
him.

4

Living in the Present

But [Lot's] wife looked back from behind him,
and she became a pillar of salt.

Genesis 19:26

Today, well lived, makes every yesterday
a dream of happiness
and every tomorrow a vision of hope.
Look well, therefore, to this day.

Attributed to Kālidāsa

In the thirties, that is, now more than fifty years ago when I was in my early twenties, I read a book by the German author Robert Musil entitled *The Man without a Character*. All I remember of the book's contents is the beginning, when the author introduces the man without a character to the reader. He says that his hero took great pride in being alive exactly at the time in which he lived, because all those who had lived before him were dead, and those who were to come after him had not yet been born. He felt superior to both his predecessors and his successors. He was proud of living in the present.

This is not the kind of present I want to consider here. What I would like to consider is rather the present that stems from the awareness that each one of us lives in the immediate, as well as in the

24

past and the future. Some say this kind of present does not exist. I believe it does. I think of this present as the edge over which the future flows into the past. The present so defined is rather ephemeral and short. But it *does* exist. Thank God. For if it didn't, we would have to invent it. We cannot think our everyday thoughts without the concepts of past, present, and future.

Animals live only in the present. For them the present is neither ephemeral nor short; it is eternal, it is the only thing they have to live in. Some hold that humans are also animals. It is a matter of definition and therefore not debatable. But animals or not, we humans live simultaneously in the past, the present, and the future.

We live in the past because we are products of the past; the past has brought us forth. And ever since Freud, at the beginning of the century, opened up the doors of the unconscious we know the vital role the past plays in our lives. But we live also in the future, an imagined future, a feared or a hoped-for future, the future of our daydreams and our nightmares. Living in the present we are the link between the past that has shaped us and the future that, at least to an extent, is shaped by us.

Out of a comparison of the present with our memory of the past and our vision of the future come many of the incentives that prod us into action. That is what makes the present relevant. For there is one thing we can do only in the present, and that is *to act*. We cannot act in the future or in the past. We can act only in the present.

> *There is a tide in the affairs of men,*
> *Which, taken at the flood, leads on to fortune;*
> *Omitted, all the voyage of their life*
> *Is bound in shallows and in miseries.*[1]

There is a tide and there is a flood of that tide. And we cannot figure out when it will occur. That moment is still in the future. And when it occurs, in the present, we must seize it. If we do not do it *then*, in *that* present, it will retreat into the past, never to come again.

Dr. Kübler-Ross, in a recent lecture, quoted this letter written by a young girl to her boyfriend:

Remember the day I borrowed your brand new
  car
and I dented it. I thought you'd kill me.
But you didn't.

And remember the time I dragged you to the
  beach
and you said it would rain—and it did.
I thought you'd say: "I told you so."
But you didn't.

And the time I flirted with all the boys to
  make
you . . . jealous, and you were. I thought
  you'd leave me.
But you didn't. . . .

And the time I forgot to tell you the dance
  was formal
and you turned up in blue jeans. I thought
  you'd smack me.
But you didn't.

And there were so many things I wanted to
  make up to you
when you came back from Vietnam.
But you didn't.[2]

A few weeks ago an old school friend of mine died. We had known each other since we were twelve years old. We grew up together. He knew my children and grandchildren and I knew his. He wrote to me after a long pause during which we had not communicated. For a reason. The contents of the letter were unimportant. But its meaning was not. It meant, let's forgive each other. I was grateful to him for taking that initiative, but found it hard to express my gratitude. I kept the letter on my desk with some other letters waiting to be answered. When he died, several weeks ago, the letter was still lying there.

The postman may ring twice but fate—as Shakespeare surmises—as a rule knocks only once with the same opportunity. If we let that opportunity slip through our fingers, are we then doomed to spend "all the voyage of [our] life . . . bound in shallows and in miseries"? I don't think so. Not by a long shot. For even if we have missed that opportunity, if we have failed to seize it, another opportunity presents itself to us. Unfailingly. That is the opportunity to accept that inadvertent failure of ours as part of our human imperfection. Our loving acceptance of our own failing self as we are now, in the present, can be an immensely creative, a redeeming act. An act that makes the future possible.

2

Believing in Miracles

5

How Miraculous Are Miracles?

Once upon a time there was a magician who
didn't know he was one because nobody ever
told him he was. . . .
    [He] lived simply . . . and worked at his job
as hard as you would expect an ordinary man
to work at an ordinary job. When one day he
died it was an ordinary sort of death. . . .
    Some time after the funeral the magician's
children discovered a diary which they did not
know their father had kept, and they opened it
and a jaguar jumped out, and yards and yards of
rainbow silk, desperate, beautiful, unwinding.

Clarke Wells
Sunshine and Rain at Once

Therefore, see without looking, hear without
    listening, breathe without asking:
The Inevitable is what will seem to happen to
    you purely by chance;
The Real is what will strike you as really absurd;
Unless you are certain you are dreaming, it is
    certainly a dream of your own;
Unless you exclaim—"There must be some
    mistake"—you must be mistaken.

W. H. Auden
"For the Time Being: A Christmas Oratorio"

I want to reflect on the concept of miracles. According to the British philosopher Richard Swinburne,

a miracle is "a violation of a law of nature by a god."[1] His definition is an abbreviated version of one offered by the Scottish philosopher David Hume, who, around the middle of the eighteenth century, defined a miracle as "a transgression of a law of nature by a particular volition of the Deity or by the interposition of some invisible agent."[2] These definitions, like the one in the *Columbia Encyclopedia*, which describes a miracle as a "departure from the usual course of nature attributed to supernatural interposition," all assign miracles to a place precariously balanced between religion and science. A god, the principal figure of religion—in the Judeo-Christian tradition, "God"—must violate something science has recognized as a law of nature. As occurrences at one time deemed to violate a law of nature may no longer appear to do so when that law of nature is refined or when new laws of nature are established, evolving science tends to eliminate many supposed miracles. The more comprehensible the universe becomes the fewer miracles have a chance to survive—but also the more credible, one could hold, the surviving miracles become.

Isaiah Berlin reports that Einstein "was totally convinced that the universe was comprehensible . . . [and that he] believed in salvation by work and more work to unravel the secrets of nature— secrets miraculously amenable to analysis and solution by human reason."[3] Only when we have unraveled all secrets of nature shall we be able to establish whether a law of nature has at any time been violated by a god, that is, whether or not miracles have really happened. Einstein's friend Chaim Weizmann, the great chemist and first president of the state of Israel, used to say: "Miracles do happen, but one has to work very hard for them."[4]

Not all twentieth-century scientists share Einstein's trust in nature's comprehensibility. Harvard physicist J. B. S. Haldane spoke for many when he declared: "My own suspicion is that the Universe is not only queerer than we suppose, but queerer than we can suppose."[5] If Haldane is correct, we may never know whether miracles have happened—that is, unless you are a believer; I mean a literalist believer. For if you believe that God created the world and everything in it, all things visible and invisible, that in his omnipotence he instituted all laws of nature, then it seems plausible to assume that he can also suspend these laws of nature, then it would be no great miracle for him to perform miracles, either directly or by delegation through some human or superhuman being.

Personally I happen to believe that God is more subtle than that. Personally I happen to believe that God need not suspend or violate any laws of nature. Personally I believe in the miracle that God performs his miracles within the framework of the laws of nature without suspending or violating any of them. That is what makes his miracles miraculous.

R. F. Holland gives an example of such a miracle:

A child riding his toy motor-car strays on to an unguarded railway crossing near his house and a wheel of his car gets stuck down the side of one of the rails. An express train is due to pass . . . and a curve in the track makes it impossible for the driver to stop his train in time to avoid any obstruction he might encounter on the crossing. The mother coming out of the house to look for her child sees him on the crossing and hears the train approaching. She runs forward shouting and waving. The little boy remains seated in his car looking

downward, engrossed in the task of
pedalling it free. The brakes of the train are
applied and it comes to rest a few feet from
the child. The mother thanks God for the
miracle . . . although, as she in due course
learns, there was nothing supernatural about
the manner in which the brakes of the train
came to be applied. The driver had fainted,
for a reason that had nothing to do with the
presence of the child on the line, and the
brakes were applied automatically as his hand
ceased to exert pressure on the control lever.[6]

We can imagine that mother, hugging her child,
thanking God for the miracle by which her little
boy was saved. Do you really believe, when she is
told later that there was nothing supernatural
about it, that the brakes of the train came to be
applied in a perfectly natural way, that she is less
grateful, or that she suddenly believes that there
was no miracle after all? I don't think so. To her it
was a miracle.

In May 1981 an article in the *New York Times* was
triumphantly heralded in the News Summary with
the following words: "A new hypothesis of the
Exodus of the Israelites from Egypt . . . attributes
the Jews' survival to natural phenomena rather
than the divine intervention claimed by the Bible."
The natural phenomena, according to Dr. Hans
Goedicke, a noted Egyptologist and chairman of the
Department of Near Eastern Studies at the Johns
Hopkins University, consisted of a volcanic eruption
at Thera, an island seventy miles north of Crete, and
a tidal wave caused by that volcanic eruption. This
tidal wave could have inundated the low coastal
lands of Egypt, which was presumably the route of
the Israelites' escape from their bondage.

Realizing that the pursuing troops of the
Pharaoh were catching up with them, the
people stopped to defend themselves on a
low plateau overlooking the sea-level desert.
As the Israelites squared off for battle, the
Egyptian chariots on the plain were wiped
out by the flash flood, while the defenders
on the height were safe.[7]

Thus established natural phenomena rather than
divine intervention would have allowed the Israelites to escape.

Dr. Goedicke's hypothesis, the result of twenty
years of analysis of a variety of archeological and
historical sources, is interesting, I'm sure, for a
number of reasons, but *not* for the reason given in
the article, namely, that "the parting of the waves
that swallowed the pursuing Egyptians . . . could
have resulted from a towering tidal wave rather
than from divine preference." For, as I see it, the
tidal wave itself could have been the instrument
of divine preference. The alternative—either tidal
wave or divine preference—is not a valid alternative. A valid alternative would be either divine
preference—executed by a tidal wave, or a hail-
storm, or the drying up of the oil in the axles of the
Egyptian chariots, or the loss of a nail in a horse's
shoe, you name it—or no divine preference. In the
latter case the tidal wave would have hit the
Egyptians purely by chance.

"The Inevitable is what will seem to happen to
you purely by chance."[8] Or as somebody said, less
poetically: "Coincidences are God's way of remaining anonymous."

And what about the greatest miracle of all, the
miracle of creation, the miracle of what happened
in the first fractions of the first second of the "big

bang"? Was the world willed—or as the book of Genesis has it, spoken—into being, or did the whole thing happen by chance? And if so, by what kind of chance? The Auden kind that fronts for the inevitable or the real chance of something happening that might just as well not have happened? And which would have been the greater miracle, the happening of creation or the nonhappening? Neither could have been a miracle if a miracle infringes on the laws of nature. Because it was the very miracle of creation that established these laws of nature. How useful can any definition of miracle be that excludes creation from the miraculous? We need some other definition of miracle, one that includes the act of creation, one that permits us to see life within the confines of natural law as the composite of miracles it is. Miracles in the sense of the unforeseen and the unforeseeable, the unexplained and the unexplainable, the uncomprehended and the incomprehensible; the miraculous in the sense of that which redeems and that which saves.

In that sense Being itself is a miracle, as are love and mercy and forgiveness. Look at your own lives, you who went to war and came back, who were persecuted and are free, who were mortally ill and are alive, you who experienced the destruction of love and found new love. But also you who accepted the destruction of love without finding new love, and those who did not return from the wars, who did not survive persecution and did not come back from the hospitals, who accepted their fate and suffered it through. For at the heart of the acceptance of suffering lies the miracle of redemption. Why this is so is part of the universal mystery.

6

Angels Unawares

Let brotherly love continue. Be not forgetful to
entertain strangers: for thereby some have
entertained angels unawares.

Hebrews 13:1–2

Alex . . . smiled. "Mother?" she said.
"Yes?"
"What about wings?"
"Well, all angels have wings."
"I mean, will I get mine right away?"
"The first day," Carol said. "And then you
can always be our guardian angel and watch
over us."

Frank DeFord
Alex: The Life of a Child

Nowhere in our Western cultural heritage do angels play as important a role as in the Christmas
story. It is the archangel Gabriel who announces to
Mary that she will bear a son "to whose kingdom
there will be no end." When he is born in the
stable, an "angel of the Lord" appears to the
shepherds to bring them "the good news of great
joy" that to them a savior is born. We sing of
"Angels we have heard on high," "Angel voices in
the heavens," and of "Him, born the king of
angels." We sing carols and tell each other stories
featuring angels, and the question arises whether
angels really do exist or whether the belief in

angels is just a superstition, one of many that make religion the hazardous enterprise it often seems to be.

The *Random House Dictionary* defines superstition as "belief not based on reason or knowledge." A troublesome definition. Because by that definition all religion would be superstition. Which, according to atheists, is exactly what religion is. But there are only few atheists among us; most of us have beliefs about the ultimate nature of things spiritual that are only in part based on reason or knowledge. Our beliefs may indeed supersede reason and knowledge. The truths we believe in may appear to us either as self-evident, in the sense in which the Declaration of Independence uses that word, truths based on nothing but their obvious validity, or they may appear to us as so complicated, so unimaginably complex (think only where modern physics is leading us) that we can speak of them only in terms of story, myth, and parable.

That is why I think that the dictionary's definition of superstition is not helpful. I would rather define superstition as the belief in things that are not true. It sounds like a simple matter to know what is true but it isn't. It may sometimes be very hard—perhaps not even possible—to establish whether something is or is not true.

I once had an experience demonstrating this ambiguity. It was during the time Ruth and I lived in our native Holland under Nazi occupation. Life in those days oscillated between normalcy and horror and the only certainty was that in the end the latter would crowd out the former, that growing horror would displace dwindling normalcy.

The apocalyptic atmosphere caused a resurgence of the belief in soothsaying and other kinds of future-revealing techniques. The word "belief" may be too strong. It was just that people in their desperation would try out anything that might reduce the suffocating apprehension of the future. I fell victim to this revival of superstition and one dark, wintry afternoon, in spite of Ruth's protestations, I visited a highly recommended old woman who lived on one of the canals in a poor section of the city and who for a modest fee would tell the future.

Her predictions were reassuring: she said that we would succeed in fleeing the country before the Nazis got hold of us. Once out of the country I would not get the job I expected to get, but another job would be waiting for me. Many months later all this turned out to be correct. Then the old woman said: I see somebody around you who is very worried, very worried about you. Her name is Anna. Do you know anybody by the name Anna? I said: "Anna is the name of my mother. She died three and a half years ago." I've never been able to forget this strange, strange incident. I have carried it with me through life like a precious stone, wondering at times whether it was genuine or fake. For I cannot place it in a religious perspective. Unless we assume that those who love us and precede us in death may become our guardian angels, as Alex's mother, on the day her little daughter died, assured her that she would get her wings right away, "the first day and then you can be our guardian angel and watch over us."[1] Who knows? Many have felt comforted and protected by loved ones who preceded them into death. What comes to mind are Hamlet's words:

There are more things in Heaven and Earth, Horatio,
Than are dreamed of in your philosophy.[2]

In any event, I do believe in angels. Two examples:

During that period of horror when I went to see the soothsayer, Ruth worked mornings in a day-care center for infants in one of the poorest neighborhoods of Amsterdam. The children came partly from Jewish, partly from non-Jewish homes. When the Nazis began rounding up Jewish families for transportation to the death camps in eastern Europe, some of the parents had gone into hiding with their children. But you cannot go into hiding with a baby whose crying might betray the whole family. It was then that some of the non-Jewish mothers offered to take in a Jewish baby. As one said (and I quote literally): "The damned Germans won't notice whether there is one child more or less in *our* family." Many of those babies were to become the sole survivors of their family. Thanks to their earthly guardian angels.

Another example: a few months ago, on a beautiful Sunday in August, I preached in Concord, Massachusetts. On the way home, when we approached the bridge, we decided to stop at a Friendly's for a cup of coffee and a sandwich. When we had finished, I took a ten-dollar bill from my wallet to pay the check at the desk and a one-dollar bill from my money clip which I left on the table as a tip for our waitress, whose name was Marcia. I put the clip back into my pocket and proceeded to the desk, ten-dollar bill in hand. I paid and we stepped out of the restaurant into the late summer heat and the noise of the heavy weekend traffic. Before Ruth could start the car, I saw somebody come running in our direction, waving as if to get our attention. It was Marcia with my wallet in her hand. "I found it on the table when I cleaned up," she said. "I thought that later in the afternoon you might miss it and be very unhappy." She was out of breath. I thought of the money—of course—but also of the multitude of credit cards, my driver's license, my Social Security card, my whole identity, and the nightmare of finding out about the loss of my wallet, later in the day, and the hassle—which would probably have been in vain—of trying to retrieve it. "You are an angel," I said and thanked her profusely. When she was gone I realized that I should at least have offered her a "finder's fee." We decided to go back to the restaurant. When we asked for her at the desk, we were told that she was going off duty and about to leave. We just got hold of her, but she refused to accept any money. "I was just cleaning off the table; that is my job," she said. We shook hands. Back in the car I said to Ruth, "She *is* an angel."

Angels, from the Greek *angelos* meaning *messenger*, according to the dictionary, are messengers of God, carriers of God's messages, especially messages addressed to human beings. To me Marcia was such a messenger, as were the women who took the Jewish babies into their homes and hearts. They showed in their behavior, their words, their deeds, their being, something of a better world, something that demonstrated how things could be as against how things are.

I said that I believe in angels. Maybe I should have said that I believe in the angelic. For Marcia is probably a very ordinary human being like most of us. She has probably done things she shouldn't have done, and omitted doing things she should have done. She probably has been angry when she should have been kind, resentful when she should have been forgiving. An ordinary human being, as were the women—certainly no saints, let me assure you—who adopted the Jewish babies. But somehow they all had that great gift of protecting and helping and touching and comforting others, that great gift of demonstrating in this life how it can be transcended, in this world how it can be overcome. Human beings carrying the angelic message. Unwinged, unrobed—just people.

There is a story of a man of the cloth who had found refuge on the roof of his house from the rising waters of a violent flood that inundated the valley where he lived. A neighbor who owned a rowboat rowed by and offered to take him along. But he said, "No, thank you, the Lord will save me." Some time later a motorboat passed by and offered a lift. But he refused with the same words: "The Lord shall save me." Then a helicopter appeared. By now our man was perching on his chimney to escape the rising waters. Once more he refused to be rescued. The Lord would rescue him. He drowned. When he entered the gates of heaven and Peter welcomed him, he could not refrain from complaining that the Lord had not rescued him. Peter was stunned: "But, good man," he said, "first we sent you a rowboat and then a motorboat and then a helicopter, but you refused to be saved." His trouble was that he did not believe in angels.

Ruth got stuck in the snow on a country road last winter when one of her tires gave out. It was in the late afternoon, a light snow was falling, and it was getting dark. A jalopy stopped and out swaggered a bearded teenager, you know, a representative of that feared, antisocial, and drug-ridden species one should try to avoid getting involved with. It took him only a few minutes to change the wheel. He refused any material expression of appreciation and gratitude, growling: "If my mom got stuck, I hope someone would do the same for her." His behavior was angelic in the sense that it implied a message about how things could be.

When Elie Wiesel received the Nobel Peace Prize, the chair of the Norwegian Nobel committee presented him with a citation, which read in part:

> Wiesel is a messenger to mankind. His message is one of peace, atonement and human dignity.

"A messenger to mankind." That comes close to the dictionary's definition of an angel. I do not believe that Mr. Wiesel *is* an angel; I do not believe that Marcia or any of the others I mentioned are angels. But I do believe that his is an angelic message, a message gleaned from his experience (as the *New York Times* puts it) "of total humiliation and of the utter contempt of humanity shown in Hitler's death camps." It was out of that experience of horror that he felt the need to meet with young German students in West Berlin and—moved by the depth of their own painful search for an understanding of the nightmarish German past—to urge reconciliation . . . between young Germans and Jews.[3]

All of us, at some time or other, have had the experience of being touched by another human being with deeds or words that carried an angelic message. All of us have that capacity to carry such messages to others. Many of you have been angels unawares, many of you have brought to others angelic messages gleaned from your own suffering and joy, winged messages, illumined by God's grace.

7

The Sanctity of the Ordinary

And it came to pass, as he sat at meat with
them, he took bread, and blessed it, and brake,
and gave to them. And their eyes were opened,
and they knew him. . . .

Luke 24:30–31

Then I realized that just such a face—a face
like all men's faces—is the face of Christ.

Ivan Sergeyevich Turgenev
Dream Tales and Prose Poems

There is this odd Sunday between Christmas and
New Year's Eve. I call it odd because, theoretically,
it should not exist. There should be no Sunday at
all between Christmas and New Year's. For our era
began with the birth of Jesus. Logically, December
twenty-fifth should be our New Year's day. But it
isn't. The birth of Jesus and the beginning of the
new year are celebrated one week apart. Why?
One can only guess. And it is my guess that
Christmas and the beginning of the new year are
too different in character to be celebrated on the
same day. For Christmas is a religious holiday,
New Year's Eve a secular one. In-between is the
transition from the religious to the secular.

I know all the clichés about the commercialization of Christmas, about the desecration of its spirituality. I cannot disagree; one cannot very well argue with the obvious. But the obvious may not do justice to the truth. For the truth of the matter is that under the surface of the nonreligious activities the spirit is at work in a thousand ways. It is important to be aware of the working of the spirit in a nonspiritual environment. Because that is where you will find it. Jesus could frequently be found in the most inappropriate places, sharing a meal with prostitutes and publicans or healing society's outcasts. It started with his birth. A manger is not the place where you would expect to find a newborn babe, certainly not a little child who was to become one of the great spiritual rulers of the world. But that is where you would have found him: in a manger. In this world the spiritual is intermingled with the secular and does not exist apart from it.

Take the annual Christmas card orgy, this mechanical and mechanized ritual. Your name is recorded on someone else's list and someone else's name on yours. The first Christmas cards were exchanged around 1845, and the habit is no doubt kept alive by the manufacturers of the millions of cards that year after year clog the channels of the mail. And still, I say, and still . . . Among the cards we receive, among the many that constitute meaningless formalities, there are without fail a few that are deeply touching, that express appreciation and encouragement, love and trust, that permit the writer to speak of his agonies and yearnings, of her joys and sorrows, and of the courage to accept the inevitable and make a new beginning when all seems to have been lost. Things of the spirit, conveyed by Christmas cards.

Christmas has a spirituality the New Year's celebration can never have. Because Christmas is about somebody else. Its secular overgrowth can never obscure the fact that it is about the birth of one who lives on, in and outside of his church, one who touches all of us, one whose example we would like to follow, one in whose ultimate solitude and suffering many of us recognize ourselves.

The solitude I have in mind is a consequence of no fault of ours. Someone loving has died, leaving the beloved enveloped in loneliness. Or someone had to accept employment far away from home, depriving loved ones of his or her presence. There may have been a divorce, perhaps justified; it was hard to live together but it may also be hard to live alone. Or illness may have created our loneliness. Such feelings of loneliness often reach an apex on holidays.

In celebrating the birth of the child, we remember the death of the man who suffered in utter loneliness, a loneliness so extreme that he felt forsaken even by his God. How unlikely that that scene of human misery would bring redemption to the world. But there was an Easter; that memory can comfort the lonely.

Turgenev tells us of a dream in which he saw himself as a boy in a small wooden church. Before him stood many people. All at once a man came up from behind and stood beside him—at once he felt that this man was Christ. He looked at his neighbor.

A face like everyone's, a face like all men's faces. . . . What sort of Christ is this? I thought. Such an ordinary, ordinary man. It can't be. But I had hardly turned my eyes away from this ordinary man when I felt again that it really was none other than

Christ standing beside me. . . . And
suddenly my heart sank, and I came to
myself. Only than I realized that just such a
face—a face like all men's faces—is the face
of Christ.[1]

Again the unlikely turns out to be true. The ordinary is discovered to be sacred. The mystery is put
together out of common material. The spirit lives in
the things of everyday.

Luke tells the story of the two disciples who on
the third day after the Crucifixion walk on the road
from Jerusalem to Emmaus. Jesus appears and
joins them. But they do not recognize him. He asks
what are they talking about. They tell him about
their master's death and his apparent resurrection.
Then Jesus, "beginning at Moses and all the
prophets . . . expounded unto them in all the
scriptures the things concerning himself." And
they still did not recognize him. Only when they
sat down to the evening meal and "he took bread,
and blessed it, and brake, and gave it to them"
were their eyes opened and they knew him. Only
in the simple, common, everyday ritual of breaking
bread and blessing it did they recognize him. Not
in the intellectual discourses, not in the discussion
of the prophets but in the ordinary, simple, trusted
gesture.

New Year's Day is also an ordinary, ordinary
day. Unless we realize that this day binds us to the
universe. For it signifies the day on which the
earth's cycle around the sun, from shortest day to
shortest day, is fulfilled, and a new cycle begun.
The days are lengthening, new hope has arisen,
new life is promised. Renewal is built into the
cosmos. The ordinary becomes sanctified.

Years ago I stood in the shadow of Stonehenge,

the mysterious configuration of huge stones on the Salisbury Plain in the south of England, thinking of the meaning of this prehistoric monument. Some modern scientists believe that it served as a huge astronomical instrument to the primitive people of that prehistoric age. One can imagine how they were terrified, year after year, by the shortening of the days. Was it possible that the days would continue to grow shorter and shorter until there would be no day left, only eternal darkness? When the sun reached its lowest zenith, the stones would cast their longest shadows in a certain unmistakable way and from there on the days should lengthen and the shadows shorten. If the shadows continued to lengthen, catastrophe would threaten. We can imagine the anxiety with which the shortest day was expected and the feelings of relief and exultation that greeted the turn-around of the cycle. The sun was still there.

Other fears have taken the place of that primitive fear. We are no longer afraid that the world will come to an end; we are only afraid that *our* world may come to an end—by our own hands. We celebrate on New Year's Eve the fact that *we* are still here; and the hope that during the coming year something will happen, something will be done to reduce the danger and give the human race a chance to fulfill its destiny. It will be a function of the spirit of the sacred in the secular. It will not be a miracle. No trumpets will sound. It will be a gathering of ordinary people, carrying briefcases, assembling at some neutral place, working out, step by step, agreements that defuse the time bomb whose fuse is presently burning. It will look like another of the unending chain of ordinary conferences, but this time it will be sanctified, the spirit will guide them, the spirit that—in Paul's words—is patient and kind, not jealous or boastful, not arrogant or rude. The spirit that does not insist on its own way, is not irritable or resentful, does not rejoice at wrong but rejoices at the right, the spirit that bears all things, believes all things, hopes all things, endures all things, the spirit of Love that never ends.

8

At Any Day,
at Any Time

*The first day of the week cometh Mary Mag-
dalene early . . . and seeth the stone taken
away from the sepulchre. Then she . . . cometh to Simon Peter and the other disciple,
whom Jesus loved, and saith unto them, They
have taken away the Lord out of the sepulchre. . . . Peter therefore went forth, and that
other disciple, and came to the sepulchre. So
ran they both together: and the other disciple
did outrun Peter, and came first to the sepulchre . . . yet went he not in. Then cometh
Simon Peter following him, and went into the
sepulchre. . . . Then went in also that other
disciple, which came first to the sepulchre, and
he saw, and believed.*

John 20:1–8

*But how the stone had been removed from the
cave's entrance—was impossible to tell. A
resurrection is always a mystery—though it
happens every day.*

David O. Rankin
"Resurrection Story," in *Portraits from the
Cross: A Meditation Manual*

Easter is preeminently the feast of renewal. In
celebrating the empty tomb we celebrate the Resurrection. The word *resurrection* is troublesome to

religious liberals. "Did the Resurrection 'really' happen?" Religious liberals have raised that question over and over again. And the answer has always been negative: "No, it can't really have happened." Today, most mainline Protestant church members as well as many Catholics would give that same answer. Many would agree with the sociologist Peter Berger that "the resurrection . . . is no longer regarded as an event in the external world of physical nature, but is 'translated' to refer to existential or psychological phenomena in the consciousness of the believer." This answer makes sense. It sounds plausible. And still . . . I think the answer is wrong. Maybe not in itself. But because it is the answer to the wrong question. For the question is not whether there was a physical resurrection. The question is what this story, regardless of whether it deals with history that has become myth or myth that has become history, *means* to us, what it has to say to us, what new truth it proclaims to us. And that new truth is the proclamation of hope for renewal and renewal of hope such as the world had not known before.

At Christmas we celebrate the mystery of light that is born out of darkness. At Easter we celebrate the mystery of life that is born out of death. The universal validity of this mystery is such that it has affected the lives of all of us, literalists and liberals, believers and unbelievers.

That is why I was so moved when I came across David Rankin's "Resurrection Story": "But how the stone had been removed from the cave's entrance—was impossible to tell. A resurrection is always a mystery—though it happens every day."

It happens every day. I know he is right. For since whatever happened on that first Easter Sunday some two thousand years ago, we have found that the Resurrection can take place on any day of the week, in any week of the year, at any place in the universe.

The high school I attended in Amsterdam was a modern—well, *then* modern—building dating from 1918, one of the features of which was a number of beautiful stained glass windows. One window adorned the landing of a stairway, an inauspicious place for so beautiful a window, especially because it bore the Latin legend *Hic Incipit Vita Nova*, "Here Begins the New Life," or more freely and possibly more accurately translated, "Here Life Is Renewed."

During the four years I spent in the upper school, I passed that window at least twice a day. I remember wondering as a boy whether they could not have found a more suitable place for this window with its compelling message. Until one day I realized that the window was placed very appropriately, for the renewal of life can take place any day, at any time, without fanfare, without incantations, so to say "in passing."

I grew up in an unchurched, secular environment in which the closest thing to the celebration of the renewal of life was New Year's Eve. Then the New Year resolutions offered an opportunity for renewal, and I remember as a boy, six, seven, eight years old, how seriously I took these resolutions and how I experienced my subsequent infringements on them, one after another, as ever so many condemnations to another year of imperfection, pending the arrival of the following New Year's Eve, after which similar disappointments would be waiting for me. It never occurred to me to disconnect the possibility of renewal from the date of December thirty-first.

In a small volume of sermons entitled *The Shaking of the Foundations*, Paul Tillich tells us of the appearance of a witness in the Nuremberg war-crime trials "who had lived for a time in a grave in a Jewish graveyard in Poland. It was the only place he—and many others—could live after they had escaped the gas chamber. During this time he wrote poetry, and one of the poems was a description of a birth. In a grave nearby a young woman gave birth to a boy. The eighty-year-old gravedig-ger . . . assisted. When the newborn child uttered his first cry, the old man prayed: Great God, hast thou finally sent the Messiah to us? For who else than the Messiah Himself can be born in a grave? But after three days the poet saw the child sucking his mother's tears because she had no milk for him. . . . After three days the child was not ele-vated to glory. . . . Probably he died, and the hope of the old Jew was frustrated once more, as it had been frustrated innumerable times before."[1]

Tillich takes this story as his point of departure into some profound theological reflections. I men-tion it here as an illustration of the expectation of renewal at the most unlikely time, in the most unlikely place. And while the expectation came to naught and hope was frustrated, there is an impli-cation of a deep awareness that renewal may take place at any time, at any place, yes, that the unlike-lihood of the place and the unexpectedness of the moment may be prerequisites for that renewal.

There is another implication: that renewal may be rooted in despair. All of us, I would venture, have had this experience or will have it sooner or later, the experience that at the bottom of despair, when everything seems to have died and there is no hope left, new life stirs and what had seemed to be an end, *the* end, turns out to be a new begin-ning. One is reminded of Luther's observation: "At the very moment it seems all lost, we are on the verge of being saved." And of Wallace Stevens's words:

After the final no there comes a yes
And on that yes the future world depends. . . .[2]

This is the process of renewal I have in mind. It does not always consist of the replacement of the old by the new. It may consist of the evolution of the old into a newness that makes the old a part of the new. The widow or widower who remarries does not forget his or her first spouse but the old marriage, in a way, lives on in the new one and in many cases strengthens it. Alcoholics who learn to abstain do not forget their alcoholism but the abstention creates a newness that derives its meaning from the memory of the addiction. It is a newness rooted in oldness.

The Lutheran book of worship contains this prayer "for young people": "Help them to take failure not as a measure of their worth but as an opportunity for a new start." A prayer for the new out of the old.

That is the newness I have been talking about. It is available to all of us at any time and at any place. Nothing can disqualify us from its grace. It is never too late; we are never too far gone. The Easter event invites us all. The Resurrection awaits us all. In it the future takes over from the past, hope from despair, the grace of the new from the ruins of the old.

3

Accepting Reality

9

The Importance of Being Known

Now there arose up a new king over Egypt, which knew not Joseph.

Exodus 1:8

And then will I profess unto them, I never knew you: depart from me, ye that work iniquity.

Matthew 7:23

Then [Peter] began . . . to curse and to swear, saying, I know not the man. And immediately the cock crew. . . . And he went out, and wept bitterly.

Matthew 26:74–75

Ruth, my wife, is a small-town person. She likes meeting people she knows, wherever she goes: at the post office, in the parking lot of the local market, and at the Town Meeting. A while ago, after a Christmas–New Year's Eve invasion of children and grandchildren (and possibly as a result thereof), our washing machine broke down. The experts decided that it had to be replaced, so Ruth went to the hardware store, selected a replacement and made arrangements for its installation. Pending the occurrence of that blessed event, she offered a down payment on the new machine, which the salesman politely declined with the words: "Oh, Mrs. Fleck, that won't be necessary, we have known you for more than twenty years." That is the kind of thing Ruth likes to hear. Of course she is aware of the mercenary component in the salesman's expression of confidence, as also of its comparative risklessness. For indeed, for more than twenty years she has trusted his advice and he her solvency, neither so far having been disappointed in the other. For twenty years they have known each other and that makes for a mutually comforting relationship. For it is comforting to know people and to be known by them.

I remember the first day after our arrival in the United States. We had left Nazi-occupied Holland on March 16, 1941. We arrived in New York, after an involuntary stay of some six weeks in Spain, on May 8. The next day we took a bus, I don't remember the destination. I do remember that I asked the driver what the fare was and that he looked at us as if we had escaped from a lunatic asylum, which, of course, in a way we had. "A nickel," he said. And I remember looking puzzled at my handful of unfamiliar coins until the driver took two nickels out of my hand, shrugged his shoulders and told us to step back. I remember thinking: "My God, I don't know a soul in this place and I am not known by a soul in this place. Anything may happen to us and nobody will care because nobody knows us." I realized that it is a frightening thing not to be known. Not to be known. I remember that the rhythm of these words reminded me of the opening bars of Beethoven's Fifth Symphony. Not to be known. Pam pam pam PAH. "That is how Fate knocks at the door," Beethoven said. Ominously. Frighteningly.

Many years later, a friend of mine who at that time was associate director of the Bureau for Study Counsel at Harvard sent me a talk she gave to a hundred or so freshmen advisers before the start of the academic year. In it she said: "Becoming known . . . is an important part of the first weeks. Students who continue to feel through freshman year that 'no one knows me' tend to suffer. . . . Being known makes a difference in and of itself— even without advice." The knowing does not have to be personal; it can be circumstantial: "He is Princeton class of 1947." "His grandfather founded the XYZ Steelworks." "Her great-grandfather died in the second battle of Bull Run."

Even scanty and erratic morsels of information like these make us feel that we can "place" that person, that somehow that person is known to us and, being known, is entitled to a degree of regard that cannot be claimed by an unknown person. Such regard miraculously saved the life of a friend of mine under the Nazi occupation of Holland. Being a Jew under Hitler's racial laws would have doomed him were it not for the fact that he was married to the daughter of a Dutch Reformed minister. He used the protection of his mixed marriage to be active in the resistance movement. One day the Gestapo arrested him and took him to headquarters. He was told to mount a flight of stairs on each step of which a human being was fastened in a way that he could not avoid stepping on them. In a room at the top of the stairs he was confronted with the head of the local Gestapo, who showed him a list of names of the members of his resistance group. He was asked whether he could explain the presence of his name on that list other than that he was a member and he said: "No." The Gestapo head said: "You understand that this means deportation to Poland with the next transport." My friend said: "Yes." Then the man consulted his file and asked: "Are you the son-in-law of the Rev. ————?" My friend said: "Yes." Whereupon the Gestapo head, with a certain pride (it sounds incredible, I know), said: "I am a deacon of my church." My friend, on a sudden impulse, realizing that he had nothing to lose, asked: "How can you, a deacon of your church, sit here and do this terrible work?" The man pressed a button, two Gestapo guards entered, took my friend away and locked him in a small room where he fell asleep. At 3:00 A.M. he was awakened. It was the Gestapo headman. "Get out," he hissed, "and don't ever show your face again." My friend got up, descended the stairs and walked home. He owed his life to the fact that the Gestapo head knew him, if only circumstantially, by association. Had he not known him in this sense, my friend would have perished, dismally.

In the Bible we find many examples of the importance of knowing and being known. One of the most ominous ones initiates the enslavement of the people of Israel in Egypt: "Now there arose up a king over Egypt, which knew not Joseph." One of the most poignant ones is Peter's denial of Jesus: three times Peter denied him: "I do not know the man." And the cock crew. "And he went out, and wept bitterly." Even had he not denied Jesus, he could not have saved him. But he could have comforted him by drawing close to him, one known and knowing face among the multitude of unknown and unknowing faces.

None of us are strangers to Peter's betrayal.

I once served on a board of trustees of a private girls' school in New Jersey. It was one of those cozy, self-perpetuating boards whose members could be, and in some cases were, reelected ad infinitum. One of these "steadies" was a middle-aged member of a well-known stockbroker's firm. In the financial crisis of the late sixties, the firm went under; it was taken over by a larger competitor but the partners, including my colleague on the school board, were wiped out. After several board meetings at which he did not appear, I asked one of his old friends—another steady—how he was. He looked over my head into space and said: "I really wouldn't know." And I realized that our former colleague, in addition to having lost his money and his position, had to suffer the indignity and misery of no longer being known by his friends.

"Then shall I know even as I am known," wrote Paul to the Corinthians. He probably referred to the relationship between human beings and God. In fact, the New English Bible translation renders these words as follows: "Then my knowledge will be whole like God's knowledge of me." But this applies equally to the relationship between human beings.

The therapist's knowing enables the patient to know. His understanding makes the patient understand. Her respect for the patient as a human being makes that patient self-respecting.

In a relationship of love there is a continuing finding out about each other, observing and discerning each other, gaining a deeper awareness of each other, which leads to an ever increasing knowing that is truly life giving. It is life giving because what becomes mutually known is each individual's uniqueness, each individual's creativity, each individual's emotional need to give and to receive.

All this happens in relationships of love between human beings.

We live by the grace of being known to others, lovingly.

We give life to others by knowing them, lovingly.

There is a reciprocity, a mutuality of knowing. And it is this mutuality that upholds life.

10

Let's Keep in Touch

*And the whole multitude sought to touch him,
for there went virtue out of him, and healed
them all.*

Luke 6:19

*The shaman . . . was licensed to practice,
dancing around the bedside, making smoke,
chanting incomprehensibilities and* touching
*the patient everywhere. The touching was the
real professional secret, always obscured by the
dancing and the chanting, but always busily
there, the laying on of hands.*

*There, I think, is the oldest and most effec-
tive act of doctors, the touching. . . . The
doctor's oldest skill in trade was to place his
hands on the patient.*

Lewis Thomas
*The Youngest Science:
Notes of a Medicine Watcher*

"Let's keep in touch." These are the words people
use when they expect to be separated by a long
distance for a long time. What they mean, of
course, is: Let's write to each other from time to
time, maybe phone occasionally, exchange birthday wishes and New Year's greetings; you know,
the works. And then the word "touch" suggests
lightness and a grandeur that seems to point to
deeper things.

Do you remember Michelangelo's painting on the ceiling of the Sistine Chapel of God awakening Adam to life? The outstretched hand of an incredibly powerful God nearly touches Adam's hand. The implication is that there has been a touching, transferring the spirit of life from God to his creature.

We speak of "a touch of genius," also of "a touch of madness." We may feel touched by somebody's actions or words when they affect the nerve center of our being. We speak of someone's having a "magic touch." When Isaiah tells how he was called to his task of prophesying, he speaks of the angel "having in his hand a burning coal . . . and he laid it upon my mouth and said, 'Behold this has touched your lips; your guilt is taken away and your sin is forgiven.' " The touch had cleansed him. In the sixties the concept of touch was vulgarized by the human potential movement. *Please Touch* was the title of a book by Jane Howard and the subtitle gave away what it was all about: *Feel Me, See Me, Know Me.* It was the vulgarization, the demonization of the concept of touch. But touch survived the corruption.

Once a month I spend a day or two in New York discharging some duties that remain from a banking career from which I retired many years ago. I stay on those occasions in a small midtown hotel, on East 65th Street to be exact. Over the years these visits to the old office have become a familiar and cherished routine.

On one of my recent trips I had a strange experience: after registering at the hotel desk, I was, as usual, taken to my quarters and began to unpack the few belongings I take along on these occasions. Suddenly I noticed that there was no television set in the room. I was in a minor panic, the kind of panic that might seize a diver when, deep under water, he notices that something is wrong with the cable that ties him to the ship on the water's surface. I called the desk and soon the TV set, which had been removed for maintenance purposes, was duly returned and reinstalled. I felt strangely relieved although I didn't look at it all evening except for the news and a few minutes of channel switching. At the same time I realized how dependent we have become on instant communication with the outside world by means none of which existed as recently as our grandparents' days.

The first of these modern means of communication was the telephone, invented by Alexander Graham Bell in 1876. In that year my father was six years old. He grew up in an essentially pretelephone world, a world of privacy within the four walls of one's home. The telephone punched a hole in one of the walls and privacy has never been the same again. Nor was the innovation accepted without problems! On the day after the telephone was installed in my grandparents' home—so my father told me—it rang with three short rings. "That must be Adele," my grandmother said, Adele being one of her less-favored nieces. "No manners and always so impatient."

I remember the preradio world. In fact, I was a foxtrotting teenager when I experienced for the first time the exhilarating sensation of dancing in Amsterdam to music of the famous band in London's Savoy Hotel. Exhilarating and somewhat dizzying because the experience upset my sense of living space, which, in spite of the earlier intrusion of the telephone, had still been limited more or less to the four walls of my house.

After the invasion of sound came the invasion of image, uninvited and, at times, inappropriate.

Once accepted, television proved to have an enriching potential. Also a foreboding one, because television threatens our sense of reality, in fact it may estrange us from reality, it may replace reality. I was told the story of a little neglected boy who had replaced his family by the characters of some serialized cartoons. When he was told to turn the TV off he protested, exclaiming, "but these are my only friends." Older people may ask visitors not to come at a certain hour because "then I have to watch my story." Not unlike the little boy, they are in touch with life vicariously through the characters in "their story."

And now it seems that the computerized home is upon us. What this means is not yet clear. According to some recent surveys, the preponderant use made of home computers is playing games, closely followed by business use, learning for children, and balancing the checkbook. But, I understand that by using the telephone lines a computer owner can leave a message on the computer of another owner and my hunch is that this communication aspect of the home computer will grow with the number of owners. Another hole in the wall that used to protect our privacy. And while we may not have welcomed these intrusions of sound and image and word, we have by now become, or are becoming, addicted to them. That became clear to me when I panicked in that hotel room because there was no television set. Originally the advent of these intruders may have disturbed us; today we feel lost without them. And you haven't seen anything yet.

"Wonders still the world shall witness," sings a hymn written in 1932 by a Unitarian minister, Jacob Trapp. And indeed, the fifty years after that hymn was written have produced more wonders than the preceding fifty, or for that matter five hundred or five thousand years, including the technical means by which we keep in touch with the world, all these antennae to the world which report to us what's going on out there and whether there still *is* an "out there" or whether, while we were asleep, the other half of the world has been blown up.

Meanwhile, as long as the world goes on, one would have thought that the means of communication would bring us closer to the outside world, closer to our fellow human beings. Wrong. These means of communication tend instead to isolate us from each other. The more communication, the more isolation. That is the strange paradox confronting us. The title of David Riesman's bestseller of the sixties, *The Lonely Crowd,* may turn out to have been a prophetic title.

Recently the British *Economist* described this increasing American individual isolationism. "There is," the author warned,

a withdrawal by Americans into their
homes. Already Americans are spending less
of their time working . . . they are spending
more time doing household repairs . . .
more time engaged in "personal care" and
sleep . . . and more time in active leisure,
presumably jogging. . . . Less time is spent
on social events . . . and more time watching
television. . . . It is not fanciful, therefore,
to see Americans in the 1980s and 1990s
withdrawing into their own homes to shelter
from the onslaughts of hard work, criminals,
parents and other predatory forces. They
are losing the taste for social events. . . .
Technology is working in the same way.
Cable and satellite television are already

bringing a large variety of programmes into American households. It is becoming possible to carry out banking and even shopping at home. Soon it may be possible to work at home, so long as you have access to the appropriate terminal. Telecommuters may never need to leave the house—except to jog.[1]

And what about church going? I wouldn't be surprised if churchgoers were already outnumbered by church-stay-at-homers, the people who watch their church service Sunday after Sunday from an easy chair in their living room, or lying in bed sipping their morning coffee. I have the feeling that they are being had, that it is not real. I don't refer to the fact that in most cases I do not believe what their preachers preach and that I suspect, in some cases, that their preachers do not believe it themselves. I refer to the fact that to be an onlooker to a church service is different from being a participant. One of a number of participants. Even ten thousand participants in a service of Billy Graham or Jerry Falwell or Kenneth Copeland, which I see on my television screen, do not make a participant of me. I remain an onlooker.

In both the Jewish and the Christian religion a mystical quality is imputed to the presence of a minimum number of participants in prayer. For the Jews it is *minyan*, ten people. With fewer than ten, no service can be held. It cannot be ten people having a conference call on the phone, or seeing each other's faces on a television screen, but ten honest-to-goodness people with their kindness and their obnoxiousness, their intelligence and their stupidity, their vision and their narrowness, their honesty and their falsehood. Real people, together in a gathering so close that they can touch each other.

The requirement of *minyan* is not biblical but talmudic, though only vaguely so. It developed in ancient time and is honored up to the present day. I see an analogy between the requirement of *minyan* and Jesus' words: "where two or three are gathered together in my name, there am I in the midst of them." It is as if he said: "You don't need ten, just two or three will do." But very clearly there has to be a number of participants, even if a small number only, who get together so close that they can touch each other before the miracle can happen, the miracle of separate people becoming a community at worship.

There are analogies in the secular world: politicians, even presidential candidates, by instinct or experience, know that the use they make of radio and television does not replace the confrontation with real people, the touch, the handshake, the embrace, the kiss. The real encounter, as against the phantom encounter on radio and television.

Phantom. Let's hold on to the word. What I am trying to say is that our lives are in danger of becoming less and less real, more and more phantomized. From the computer's voice telling me that I misdialed and should try again to the TV character from my favorite soap opera who has become my best friend, it is all part of a process of fantasy. Sometimes we protest.

Henry Wriston, the former chairman of the National City Bank, decreed one day that clients having less than $5,000 in their checking account would henceforth no longer have access to real tellers (people, that is) but would have to transact their business through machines. The small depositors revolted and Mr. Wriston had to rescind his little plan. I tell the story to illustrate that there is in us an instinct for reality. Although the story may also illustrate something else: suppose that Mr. Wriston had reserved the infallible machines for the large depositors and had arranged for the small ones to be served by fallible human tellers. In that case the small depositors might have revolted against the human tellers. I don't know. But I do know that slowly our lives are in danger of being dehumanized, that the realness is taken out of it, that the phantom is about to take over, that the means of communication threaten to become barriers against communication.

I said earlier that there may be deeper meanings in writing letters and birthday cards and making occasional telephone calls. Deeper things. Mysterious things. Let me describe my own experience, which, I am sure, I share with many others.

There are a number of people of whom I think every day. "Think" may be too strong a word, for I do not consciously devote specific daily thoughts to them. It's more that they are somehow on my mind so that they, or rather my thoughts of them, have become a part of me. On quite a few occasions, especially during the last few years, I have met with friends I had not seen for many years—in one specific case, for more than forty-five years—during which I had carried thoughts of them along with me, as they, who knows, may have carried along thoughts of me. Invariably these reunions were characterized by an astonishing and unexpected ease with which we picked up where we had left off twenty, thirty, forty-five years ago. It was as if through thought we had stayed in touch.

In 1940 we lost our first-born, an apparently healthy little boy, who stayed with us but five days. Our memory of him is deeply anchored in our thoughts but we think of him no longer as a baby. He has grown up and grown older in our thoughts. He has remained part of our lives, although in a way different from if he had lived. We have the feeling that we kept in touch.

In the three synoptic Gospels the word "touch" appears thirty times. In John's Gospel only once, and then in a negative sense, when Jesus says to Mary Magdalene, "Touch me not for I am not yet ascended to my Father." I believe that this discrepancy has a deep significance: In John's Gospel, Jesus is no longer the divinely inspired rabbi of the synoptic Gospels who moved among and touched his people, but a hellenistic, godlike being, distant, remote, out of touch.

In the synoptics, the touching is on various occasions initiated by believers, as in Matthew 14:36 when they

> brought unto him all that were diseased;
> and besought him that they might only
> touch the hem of his garment: and as many
> as touched were made perfectly whole.

More often it is Jesus who takes the initiative, as in Matthew 8:15 when he heals Peter's mother-in-law: "He touched her hand and the fever left." Or earlier in the same chapter when he heals the leper:

> And Jesus put forth his hand and touched
> him, saying . . . be thou clean. And
> immediately his leprosy was cleansed. (8:3)

The story that they brought him little children "that he should touch them" occurs in all three synoptic Gospels and in all three Jesus makes the point that "of such is the Kingdom of Heaven." Matthew mentions, in addition, "he laid his hands on them. . . ." Mark goes all out: "And he took them up in his arms, put his hands upon them, and blessed them" (10:16). Yet the majority of cases in which Jesus touches people, or allows them to touch him, concern cures. There are so many examples. I take one more from the fourth chapter of Luke:

> Now when the sun was setting, all they that had any sick with divers diseases brought them unto him; and he laid his hands on every one of them, and healed them. (4:40)

We religious liberals are supposed to be devoted to the rationality of science, as of course we are, and to look with contempt on superstitions such as healing by mere touch, as of course we do. I know my liberal catechism. And I confess that I might not have dared talk of healing had it not been for the encouragement I found in Lewis Thomas's book *The Youngest Science: Notes of a Medicine Watcher:*

> Today many patients go home speedily, in good health, cured of their diseases. In my father's day this happened much less often, and when it did, it was a matter of good luck or a strong constitution. When it happens today, it is . . . frequently due to technology. . . . The close-up, reassuring, warm touch of the physician, the comfort and concern, the long leisurely discussions in which everything including the dog can be worked into the conversation, are disappearing from the practice of medicine, and this may turn out to be too great a loss for the doctor as well as for the patient.[2]

What Thomas says here, I think, is clear: blessed be the incredible advances made by the medical sciences, the apparatus, the machines, the computers, and what not. But let us try to preserve at least a modicum of the personal relationship between doctor and patient, including the physical closeness. Let's stay in touch, he seems to say, for it is the loving physical touch expressing spiritual closeness that can, by God's grace, console the crying, comfort the lonely, and give peace to the dying.

11

Taking a Rest

*And on the seventh day God ended his work
which he had made; and he rested on the
seventh day from all his work which he had
made. And God blessed the seventh day, and
sanctified it: because that in it he had rested
from all his work which God created and made.*

Genesis 2:2–3

*For thus saith the Lord God, the Holy One of
Israel: In returning and rest shall ye be saved;
in quietness and in confidence shall be your
strength. . . .*

Isaiah 30:15

*A carpenter and his apprentice were walking
together through a large forest. And when
they came across a tall, huge, gnarled, old,
beautiful oak tree, the carpenter asked his
apprentice: "Do you know why this tree is so
tall, so huge, so gnarled, so old and beautiful?" The apprentice looked at his master and
said: "No . . . why?" "Well," the carpenter
said, "because it is useless. If it had been
useful it would have been cut long ago and
made into tables and chairs, but because it is
useless it could grow so tall and so beautiful
that you can sit in its shade and relax."*

Tao story

By the first of September the end of summer is in
sight. The high point of the vacation and tourist

74

season is over. Most people return to school or work after Labor Day, but for many of us Cape Cod dwellers it means that the busiest period of the year is coming to an end, both for those who make a living supplying services that bring the tourists here, and for those who have been providing memorable summer vacations for children, grandchildren, and friends. For them Labor Day does not spell the end but the beginning of vacation. For it is only then that they can begin to recover from the ravages of the summer onslaught.

It is good to take a vacation. It is also a sign of an ordered life. The unemployed do not take vacations. Nor do those who are apprehensive about the future, who feel that for some reason or other their way of life is threatened. For not only does it take a degree of health and wealth to go on vacation; it also takes a degree of light-heartedness and carefreeness. Come to think of it, I would not be surprised to find that the number of vacationgoers comprises only a comparatively small percentage of the total population.

The God-given day of rest, however, is shared by all:

And he rested on the seventh day from all
his work which he had made. And God
blessed the seventh day and sanctified it,
because that in it he had rested from all his
work which God created and made.

That is how the Sabbath came into existence. In Exodus the day of rest becomes a covenant between the people of Israel and God:

Six days may work be done; but in the
seventh is the sabbath of rest, holy to the

> Lord. . . . Wherefore the children of Israel
> shall keep the sabbath . . . throughout their
> generations, for a perpetual covenant. It is a
> sign between me and the children of Israel
> forever: for in six days the Lord made
> heaven and earth, and on the seventh day
> he rested, and was refreshed. (31:15–17)

Anthropologists might give a different explanation of the cycle of rest. Animals, so some have reasoned, spend their waking hours foraging for food. Apart from continuing the species, that is their sole activity in life. Only when the human animal so improved the methods of food gathering that some members of the clan could be excused from this search to assume higher duties as priests or secular rulers, only then did a human society emerge. The Sabbath can be seen as a more just and democratic version of this process: the free days are no longer limited to a few but in Israel as a nation all of its members, regardless of their social standing, masters and servants, slave owners and slaves, all are to observe the weekly holiday as God observed it at the beginning.

The early church switched the weekly day of rest from Saturday to Sunday, from the last day of the week to the first day of the week, from the commemoration of the creation to the commemoration of the Resurrection. "Already in the year 321 [the emperor] Constantine had issued a decree which was to eliminate the observance of the Jewish Sabbath from Christian life. . . . [It] reads as follows: 'All Judges and common people of the city and workers in all the crafts are to rest on the holy Sunday.' "[1] In 326 the Council of Nicea confirmed this decree. Still, the Jewish tradition apparently maintained itself for "a quarter of a century later—

at the Council of Laodece another resolution had to use very harsh language. 'The Christians,' it said sternly, 'must not judaize and sit idly on the Sabbath, but ought to work on that day. They must honor the Lord's Day . . . by resting inasmuch as they are Christians. But if they persist in being Jews, they ought to be anathema to Christ.' "[2] With these prohibitions against the Christian observance of the Jewish Sabbath, Christianity severed one of the last remaining bonds with its parent religion.

Meanwhile the synagogue and the church developed a network of religious holidays that provided a satisfactory rhythm within the Western work pattern, until the industrial revolution altered that pattern. It created a need for a vacation period, that is, a number of consecutive days with no special religious or secular duties for the individuals, a number of days wholly their own—a break in the monotony of fulfilling their industrial tasks.

An agricultural society requires no such vacations. The change of the seasons weaves recurring periods of rest into the fabric of the farmer's life; farmers do not go on vacations. However, since the industrial revolution, the percentage of our population that lives on farms has decreased from eighty percent to three percent. Most of us, therefore, need vacations beyond the religious and secular holidays that dot our calendar.

To the very young, vacations can be confusing. In the primary school I attended, we had six weeks' summer vacation. Oh, it seemed eternity. Six weeks at a very young age is forever. That is how I experienced it. And when we came home after spending those six weeks somewhere in the mountains or at the seashore, I found that I had to rediscover many things of my daily life. For a very young child forgets a lot in six weeks.

And now I live in a place where other people come to spend their vacation. And in order to have a vacation I have to go somewhere else. A real vacation, for most people, presupposes a change of environment. I know people who live at the Cape all year round but for their vacation they go to Boston, New York, or London, to spend their days in the museums, their evenings at the theater, feeding themselves in between in all kinds of fancy restaurants. For these people, an important aspect of their vacation is the increase in options, the increase in choices of how to spend their days. Others want to spend their vacations in places where the number of choices is reduced.

A colleague of mine from Wall Street days used to take his vacation all by himself, away from his family. He would have himself flown out to some deserted lake in the barrenness of northern Newfoundland, left there for two weeks with some cans of food, his fishing gear, and a rifle. Then the plane would pick him up and fly him home, where he would don his three-piece suit and on Monday morning appear in the office, refreshed.

Of course, these are two extremes, the London-goer and the Newfoundland-camper, the one looking for a maximum, the other for a minimum of options. Most of us want something in-between.

Twice in recent years Ruth and I have spent a week on Star Island in the Isles of Shoals off the Maine–New Hampshire coast, that blessed place of reduced options. No choice of TV programs because there is no TV. No choice of radio programs because there is no radio. No choice of places to eat or dishes to order. No question whether to go somewhere by car or by bus because there are no cars and no busses and no places to go. But, oh . . . the discoveries one makes about the seagulls and the tides and the people and about oneself. I believe that one of the ways to find rest is to give up options, to abstain from doing things rather than doing them.

Rest can be found in the most unexpected ways, in the most unlikely company. Many years ago we knew a family, mother, father, and five children, one of whom, a little girl, was born brain-damaged. She could not sit up and was unable to speak. She died before reaching adolescence. She spent her apparently useless short life lying in bed in the sunniest room of the house at the top of a short flight of stairs, just above the living room. Several times during the day one or the other member of the family, parent or child, would go up to the girl's room and keep her company. When she died people said it was a blessing. But the family was devastated; they mourned her for a long time. We asked the mother, "Why does the death of this child who has never spoken or moved among you make you all feel so deeply bereft?" "You don't understand," was the answer. "Whenever one of us was sad or happy, joyful or depressed, we would go to her room and laugh or cry or just put our head on the pillow next to hers. The room was always quiet. When we left we would feel restored." "But she could not even speak," I said. "That's right," her mother answered, "she could not even speak."

I've never forgotten the story of that little sick girl and her apparently useless life in whose presence her parents, her brothers and sisters and their friends found rest and felt restored. What happened, I think, was that in the presence of that child the persons who sought her company relaxed, let go, and got in touch with their inner being, with their souls. That may be the ultimate process of resting: not to travel, not to go out and do things, not to spend our time in what we deem to be "useful" ways, but rather to let go, to open ourselves up to the spirit, to get in touch with our soul.

Walt Whitman wrote:

> *I loafe and invite my soul,*
> *I loafe at my ease, observing a spear of summergrass.*[3]

In these lines I detect an echo of the biblical account of the Sabbath's origin: "on the seventh day he rested." That means he didn't do a single thing all day, he let it go to waste! "And was refreshed."

12

The Denial of Reality

Quantum theory . . . works. But it has three
very peculiar features:

- Its predictions take the form of stating
  probabilities rather than unique out-
  comes.
- It treats uncertainty . . . as an intrin-
  sic feature of the subatomic world.
- It even suggests that an observer and
  the event, or object, he observes cannot
  always be regarded as distinct. . . .

Of course, this opens Pandora's box. If subatomic objects "exist" only when they are
being observed—if the object and the observer
are not independent of one another—what
about the larger objects of everyday life, which
themselves are made up of subatomic particles? Some scientists say you have to accept
that the existence of these larger objects, too, is
not independent of an observer. Others deny
this and say the common-sense view of reality
still holds when it comes to tables and chairs.

The Economist, 26 September 1981

The man bent over his guitar,
A shearsman of sorts. The day was green.

They said, "You have a blue guitar,
You do not play things as they are."

The man replied, "Things as they are
Are changed upon the blue guitar,"

And they said then, "But play, you must,
A tune beyond us, yet ourselves,

A tune upon the blue guitar
Of things exactly as they are.''

Wallace Stevens
"The Man with the Blue Guitar"

I have always wondered why so many high posi-
tions in our society are filled by people of mediocre
intelligence. Take the presidency of the United
States, a position than which none is more illustri-
ous, more awesome, more revered, certainly in
this country, possibly in the world at large. Still,
one has to admit that since the death of John
Kennedy, few, if any, of our presidents have been
intellectual giants.

I know people, ordinary people, bankers, law-
yers, ministers, teachers, whose intelligence I rank
higher than that of several of those presidents.
Does that mean they would have made better
presidents? Not necessarily. For there are other
qualifications than intellectual prowess that determine eligibility for the White House. One of these,
I believe, is the ability to accept reality, even the
most adverse reality, without quarreling with it.

I am a quarreler with reality. If reality is not to
my liking, I fight it. Invariably, I lose the fight. Of
course. But not before I have squandered immense
energy on the struggle. First, by denying that
reality, as if my denial could wipe it out, and then
by remaking it in my mind into something more to
my liking, something that is less troubling, causes
less anguish, less pain. Until, in the end, I recognize that reality's factualness can in the long run be
denied only at the cost of one's sanity.

The denial of reality. I remember my reaction to
the news of President Kennedy's assassination. I
was having a hasty luncheon in a drugstore some-

where in uptown Manhattan before taking a cab to my downtown office. Sitting at the counter, I heard the radio blare a story about an assassin who shot the president and I remember thinking, "They should not broadcast such stories that people might mistake for truth," vaguely recalling Orson Welles's broadcast about a Martian invasion, which had alarmed a national radio audience in 1939. I paid the check, went out and hailed a cab. Before I could give him my destination, the driver turned around and said: "The president is dead." All I could say—I remember it distinctly, I still hear myself saying it, three times—was: Oh no, oh no, oh no.

The denial phase did not last long. Reality prevailed. But, even now, after many years, I fight occasional rearguard actions against it, imagining how things might have been if a different reality had prevailed. The lingering illusion that reality can be bargained with, that one can make a deal with fate, disqualifies me from the presidency of the United States. I console myself with the realization that, being foreign born, I am not eligible anyway.

I use the word *reality*, though I have often entertained and expressed serious doubt about reality's ultimate reality. Indeed, I think it is full of holes, yes, in the end it may turn out to be more hole than anything else. Modern physics seems to support my doubts. In his book *Other Worlds*, the physicist Paul Davies, whose credentials are impeccable, comes to the conclusion that " 'objective reality' is an illusion"[1] and that "there is [no] . . . agreement among physicists . . . either on the nature nor existence of reality. . . ."[2] Fritjof Capra, in his book *The Tao of Physics*, reports that subatomic physics has "called in question the very foundation of the mechanistic world-view—the concept of the reality of matter."[3]

Yet who can deny that on the level of our individual existence, on an existential level, there *is* a reality. It may be true that my armchair near the fireplace, at the subatomic level—to quote Capra again—"dissolve[s] into wavelike patterns of probabilities"[4] but that will not prevent me from settling into its inviting contours in the confidence that it is really there and spending many evenings sitting in it, reading, or just looking into the fire. To me that chair is a tremendous reality. Like food and drink and love and going sailing.

When I am hungry or thirsty or sick, it is real. Our daily lives consist of realities: I passed my bar exam or I flunked it. I got tenure or I didn't. I married my sweetheart or she ran off with some other guy. I inherited a million dollars or that great-uncle of mine left it to his girlfriend. Somebody lost his young wife. Somebody else is an alcoholic. Somebody's child suffers from Down's syndrome. The doctor told me that I have one more year to live. No, *he* escaped the Nazis; it is his *brother* they killed. Or, he's been dead for many years, he disappeared in Vietnam, or, he is dying of AIDS. These are realities of existence, desperate realities. I could go on. And the longer I were to go on, the clearer it would become that these realities that together form fate, the fate of an individual or of a group of individuals, are in part realities about which we can do something, that we control, and in part realities about which we can do nothing, that are beyond our control. The demarcation line between the two is hard to establish. And then again, there may be a deeper truth: for isn't it true that by accepting the unchangeable, we do change it? Accepting it not in a fatalistic spirit of resignation, but as a prelude to action, to doing some-thing, not *about* it for that is impossible, but *with* it.

In her book *The Child Who Never Grew*, Pearl Buck describes her heartbreak when she learned that her little daughter was retarded. She recounts the painful odyssey on which she embarked with her child through doctors' offices around the world in search for a remedy that did not exist. She de-scribes how in the meantime "the process of ac-commodation began. The first step," she writes, "was acceptance of what was. Perhaps it was consciously taken in a day. Perhaps there was a single moment in which I actually said to myself 'This thing is unchangeable, it will not leave me. No one can help me, I must accept it.' But practi-cally the step had to be taken many times."[5] She did accept the unchangeable. She raised her daughter carefully and lovingly. When the child was ten years old she decided that the time had come to entrust her to an institution where she would be able to live a protected life together with others who shared her fate.

During these years Pearl Buck adopted nine other children. In 1949 she founded Welcome House, an adoption agency that finds homes for children of mixed Asian-American heritage. She comforted and guided, through private counsel-ing, through a voluminous correspondence, and through her books, thousands of parents, and children who were retarded, orphaned, or of mixed racial lines. All this she did *with* the un-happy reality of her own daughter's illness *about* which she could do nothing.

A few years ago, just before election day, we saw Senator Edward Kennedy on TV, delivering a speech, surrounded by members of his family. At his side was a young man with a radiant expression on his handsome face. It was the Senator's older son Ted, who, as a youth, had lost one leg to cancer. The illness, obviously, was a reality *about* which nothing could be done. But father and son must have done something *with* it, something that made the young man's face shine with this beautiful radiance. Yet, before being able to do anything *with* that reality they must both have found the courage to confront it, they must both have been able to overcome the "oh no" phase of denial and accept its shattering implication: the necessity of an amputation.

I'm reminded of the biography of Bobby Massie, written by his parents, the authors Robert and Suzanne Massie. In his infancy he was discovered to have hemophilia. It was his parents' and his unquestioned acceptance of this adverse reality that permitted him to lead a normal life that comforted and encouraged many other sufferers of hemophilia. I remember a picture of him in a wheelchair while he was a student at Princeton; his face showed a radiance similar to that of the Kennedy boy. His biography[6] consisted of chapters written by his father, his mother, and by himself. All three accepted the unchangeable and did something with it.

Children are realists. Some years ago a granddaughter of ours shared a room in Boston's Children's Hospital with a seventeen-year-old victim of cystic fibrosis, who knew that her life expectancy was limited. (Think of it—at age seventeen!) For her that was a reason "to make every moment count." These were her words. One day when Ruth was sitting in their room, waiting for the outcome of tests done on our granddaughter, the seventeen-year-old, sensing her worry, turned to Ruth and said: "You don't get many options, do you?" Indeed you don't!

I could give many more illustrations of the good things, the creative things people have done *with* adverse realities they accepted because it was impossible to do anything *about* them. So, I'm sure, could you, especially those among you who themselves have consciously walked the rocky road between the denial and ultimate acceptance of disastrous reality.

But then there are those who cannot accept that reality, who will persist in their denial. They live in an unreal world of fantasy, often maintained by excessive indulgence in sex, alcohol, or drugs.

Some of you may have seen or read Edward Albee's play *Who's Afraid of Virginia Woolf?* You will remember how Martha and George, the middle-aged, childless couple, torture each other, in the presence of a younger couple throughout a night of drinking and sex, with the fate of their imaginary son. The son, supposedly away at college, is expected home the next day to celebrate his twenty-first birthday. Or at least that is what they, the quasi-parents, tell each other and the younger couple who have no reason to disbelieve the story. But George realizes that the fantasy, once it has been shared with two outsiders, can no longer be maintained. He shatters the long-indulged-in unreality by announcing that earlier that night the postman had delivered a telegram to him, advising the parents of their son's death in an automobile accident. By killing their imaginary son, George tries to find the road back to reality. But Martha resists vehemently. She cannot face the reality of her unhappy, childless marriage. In the last scene, George recites the requiem while Martha bemoans her son. The young couple begin to understand and depart, leaving the older couple alone in the agony of their quasi-bereavement. Morning dawns. And then with very few words, inter-rupted by long silences, they begin to try to find their way back to reality, together. Maybe they will succeed, maybe they will not. Maybe it's too late. Maybe it isn't. I believe it never is.

4

Making a
Choice

13

The Willingness to Be Disturbed

What doth it profit, my brethren, though a man say he hath faith, and have not works? can faith save him? If a brother or sister be naked, and destitute of daily food, and one of you say unto them, Depart in peace, be ye warmed and filled; notwithstanding ye give them not those things which are needful to the body; what doth it profit? Even so faith, if it hath not works, is dead, being alone.

James 2:14–17

One of the distinguishing features of liberal theology . . . is the constant concern for social justice as a religious and not merely a secular matter. Nothing makes a theological liberal more angry than the suggestion that religion is a matter of the privacy of the heart only, that genuine religion, understood as deep personal experience, has no direct bearing on questions of justice, equality and freedom in society.

Max Stackhouse
Introduction to James Luther Adams,
On Being Human Religiously

Inner harmony. Is there anybody who does not aspire to it? Is there anybody who does not strive for it? Indeed, the quest for personal inner harmony in our society has kept pace with the growth of society's disharmony.

Peace of Mind and *Peace of Soul* were typical titles of best-selling books during the fifties;[1] in the sixties came the guru cults, the meditation techniques, yoga, the drug counterculture, the communes, and the revival of evangelicalism, very diverse movements that had in common, I believe, an escapist attitude of its adherents who desired to find peace of mind, to create an island of contentment within an ocean of discontent, a refuge of inner peace within the turmoil and chaos of wars and rumors of wars. They were pietistic refugees from the confusion of society's tribulations. And here lies the rub. Pietists turn their backs on the world and pursue inner harmony as an ideal in itself. But what is the value of an individual's inner harmony and peace of mind if it cannot be shared with others? Napier and Whitaker say in their book *The Family Crucible*:

> We doubt that lasting satisfaction can be had in single-minded pursuit of the self. What is needed is a balanced sense of Self *and* Others in some meaningful relation. To achieve that sense of balance, we believe that people must struggle together—lover with lover, husband with wife, parent with child, child with child. . . .[2]

Inner harmony as a goal in itself is not an effective means to engage in such struggle.

Some years ago I saw a television documentary on welfare administration. It showed glimpses of how the huge bureaucracy grinds out its meager subsidies to the poor and needy, how the individual recipient is caught—and frequently becomes lost—in a maze of forms and questionnaires, of buildings, corridors, offices, information desks and waiting rooms, how, in the words of the apostle James's letter, the poor are dishonored by the process in spite of the fact that, as the television documentary made clear, many welfare workers try to be humane to their clients. But the system does not lend itself to humaneness: a client is not an equal or a friend. And while one shudders to think what our society would be without the institution of welfare, one cannot help but wonder why it is not possible for the government, first to conduct its business with less partiality—to use James's words—and second, to conceive an altogether different and more just system that respects the recipient's dignity, and, ultimately, to evolve a social system from which poverty—at least in its crudest form—is altogether eliminated. An evolution from a very imperfect system of mercy to a less imperfect system of justice.

Why, I wondered, had I never thought of this before, why had I never cared? Frankly, because I had never realized what it feels like, what it *is* like, to be a recipient of welfare. I had never known. And how can you care if you don't know?

Several years ago I set out to raise money for the Cape Cod Family and Children's Service, Inc., whose board I chaired at that time. It was difficult to convince prospective donors of the need. When I told them that Barnstable county has the highest divorce rate in the commonwealth, that the rate of alcoholism on the Cape is one of the highest in the nation, that the use of drugs is pervasive, that child abuse and wife battering abound, I saw on their faces a mixture of disbelief and annoyance at my effort to break down the protective walls of their ignorance.

Protective, for the fact of the matter is that most of us are *not* impervious to the suffering of others; if we knew about it, it would disturb us. And who wants to be disturbed? For disturbance threatens our inner harmony. So we prefer not to know.

The unwillingness of many people to be disturbed by the knowledge of other people's suffering is one of the reasons why in recent centuries—as the theologian Max Stackhouse observes—only a minority of churches have attempted to articulate the principles of God's righteousness for the economic order. The majority of churchgoers have been otherwise preoccupied. They go to church to gain inner harmony, peace of mind, comfort and strength, or to thank God for blessings bestowed, not to speak of more mundane reasons for church attendance. The majority go to church for reasons pertaining to what James Luther Adams has called "the privacy of the heart."

Meanwhile the church has found itself in the predicament of catering to constituencies whose needs are ultimately in conflict—the minority of churchgoers who, risking their inner harmony, are willing to be disturbed by knowledge of the suffering of others and who are willing to translate their disturbance into action, social action, and the majority of churchgoers who, preoccupied with inner harmony, pay, at best, lip service to the needs and suffering of others. This majority fits Adams's definition of pietists: they restrict religion to the "immediate relations between the individual and God. In pietism," he wrote, "the relation to God is a one-to-one relation between the individual soul and God." It is these pietists who, in James's words, "have faith but have not works."[3] They do not know and do not want to know. They are not disturbed. The search for inner

harmony that excludes the other becomes a demonic enterprise.

Pietism can also be expressed in the relationship
between the individual and other individuals, that
is—as Adams puts it—"with the other Saints,"[4]
with the chosen few, chosen by *me*, those who
think as I do, live as I do, who are well clad and
well fed as I am, who do not disturb my inner
harmony with questions of justice, equality, and
freedom. Theirs is the relationship of partiality
against which James warns: "If you show partiality, you commit sin."

Is there indeed an implicit conflict between inner
harmony and concern for, compassion with, the
other? I believe there is. But the effort to resolve
that conflict may lead to the height of human
spirituality. The redemptive quality of the Gospel
story lies in the fact that it presents a solution to
that conflict. Some human beings find inner harmony in compassionate involvement with the
other. Fresh in my memory is a movie about
Mother Teresa, the incredible woman who works
among the destitutes and lepers in India and AIDS
victims in the United States. What a shining example of inner harmony shared with and bestowed
upon others and in turn derived from her preoccupation with others. What a faith converted into
works. At one moment she would caress the sick
and a minute later, with the same radiance, decree
how many toilets the new extension of the hospital
would need. How much evil can be redeemed by
such inner harmony, shared with others.

She is one of a multitude in every generation; a
small minority, yes, but still a multitude. Schweit-
zer was one of them and Florence Nightingale and
Saint Francis and numerous others who comfort
and encourage and enable, who find strength in

giving of their own strength to others, joy in sharing their joys with others, who suffer with the sufferers and mourn with the mourners. They are the salt of the earth and the vanguard of the Kingdom.

14

Misusing Our Power

*So God created man in his own image . . .
male and female created he them. And God
blessed them, and God said unto them, Be
fruitful, and multiply, and replenish the
earth, and subdue it: and have dominion . . .
over every living thing that moveth upon the
earth.*

Genesis 1:27–28

*And Jesus . . . was led by the Spirit into the
wilderness, being forty days tempted of the
devil. And in those days he did eat nothing:
and when they were ended, he afterward
hungered. And the devil said unto him, If thou
be the Son of God, command this stone that it
be made bread. And Jesus answered him,
saying, It is written, That man shall not live
by bread alone, but by every word of God.*

Luke 4:1–4

In our civilization power has a doubtful reputation.
Lord Acton's statement to the effect that "power
corrupts and absolute power corrupts absolutely"
is not only overquoted but the point is overstated.
I, for one, would not agree that power necessarily
corrupts. I subscribe to Reinhold Niebuhr's words,
written one generation after Lord Acton's: "Power
is not evil in itself."[1] But the second part of Lord
Acton's admonition, that "absolute power corrupts

absolutely," has been found true, time and again throughout history, and especially in this blood-drenched century. It was true one generation ago of Mussolini, Hitler, and Stalin, as it is true today of the Ayatollah Khomeini, of Qaddafi and the rulers of a number of other countries.

One could hold that a democratic system has one principal objective: to prevent power from becoming absolute, and thereby corruptive in any part of the body politic, by breaking power in pieces, as many pieces as there are adult citizens in the nation. Through our voting system every citizen can delegate part of that power to the political structures of government, local, state, and federal, which culminate in the three branches of government, legislative, judicial, and executive, forming ultimately a system of checks and balances that, from its very inception, has protected this nation from the vicissitudes of absolute power and thereby has preserved its liberty.

All the individuals who make up this government, from the president down to the town dog-catcher, have power—unequal but not unlimited. The Ayatollah's and Qaddafi's power, on the other hand, is unlimited; it is absolute and, in consequence, tends to corrupt absolutely.

I want to distinguish between two concepts of power, the large-scale, or macropower—both the limited kind of the president of the United States and the unlimited kind of the Ayatollah—and small-scale, or micropower, wielded by individuals, which thrives in a democracy and which may well be its earmark. It is the power of the president of the small corporation, the department head or the faculty member at the university, the scientist in charge of the lab, the head nurse at the hospital, the local policeman, the prison warden. It includes the power of the greater and smaller hierarchies, the power that holds the military forces together, the crew of the smallest fishing boat, and the crew of the most sophisticated space shuttle. It is the power that permeates the clergy and emanates from it in the form of influence or authority or prestige. It includes remnants of the power husbands used to exert over their wives, and in certain respects still do, if only because they tend to be physically stronger than their wives. And, of course, it includes the virtually absolute power parents have over their young children. Each one of us has some power over somebody, rightly or wrongly, directly or indirectly.

I believe that one of the greatest sins we can commit—and I use the old-fashioned word "sin" rather than the word "mistake" or shortcoming or immaturity or neurosis—is to use the power we have over others to our own advantage.

This is the deeper meaning of the story of Jesus' temptation in the wilderness as told in Luke's Gospel: the devil tries to persuade Jesus to use his power to his own benefit; and—at the price of worshiping the devil—to gain power over all the kingdoms of the world and the glory thereof. But he said, no, my power will be used for the benefit of those over whom I have power, all of it, leaving me powerless with regard to my personal interests and my personal fate.

We are sometimes unaware of the implications of our macropower. "Fill the earth and subdue it," God said to Adam, and that is what we have done. Having used our power to subdue the earth to our advantage without considering the consequences, we now live in a subdued but polluted world. We are at times also unaware of our micropower: some youth may have chosen us as a substitute mother or father, or conversely an elder person may see in us a substitute daughter or son. In our ignorance we may misuse these persons' dependency on us for our benefit.

Take our children. Upon birth they enter into our power; our children's emancipation from that power is part of the essential process of growing up and becoming independent individuals. In fact, one might define the process of raising children as the use of one's absolute power over the child to teach the child to overcome that power and become independent of it. Totally. Without strings attached. And to do that without the use of violence.

In an issue of a woman's journal dedicated to family violence an article appeared by a young woman who had committed the inexcusable mistake of letting her husband teach her how to drive. When for the third time she made the same error in the manual handling of the gearshift, he reached over and slapped her hand. "I reacted instantaneously and violently," she wrote,

> slamming on the brakes, screaming at him and threatening never to drive with him again. He was speechless, protesting that all he had done was to slap my hand. But I was not overreacting. It seemed to me that I had been physically violated by that simple act of his.[2]

When a few years later she became a parent, she also became a hand slapper and worse. And she wondered: "how could the slapped so easily become a slapper?" In partial reply, she quotes the old story of husband hitting wife who hits the child who hits the younger child who hits the dog. She wonders: When does physical abuse become physical violence? The first time she spanked her child, she writes, "I realized . . . it is anger, it is a desire for deterrence, it is desire to be a good parent, it is desire to have power over someone."[3] A desire to have power over someone. There it is. The old sin. The use of power over another human being to one's own satisfaction. With admirable honesty, she writes: "I know that the seeds of violence are within *me*."[4] The desire to have power over someone else violates the other's self-esteem, the other's dignity, yes, the other's sacredness, regardless of whether the other is one's spouse, one's child, one's friend, or one's enemy.

One could hold, I think, that every encounter between humans contains the elements of a subconscious, if not conscious, play for control. Del Martin, in her book *Battered Wives*, tells us about a former highway patrol officer: "When he first went on patrol and saw his fellow officers roughing up suspects he would flinch. But after a while he became so calloused that the sight no longer bothered him. At that point he knew it was time to quit. It is my guess," she concludes, "that he got out just in time. Someone who is immune to the pain of others is, in my estimation, most dangerous."[5] The culture that prides itself on such immunity to the pain of others is that of the devil.

"The pain of others." I read in the *New York Times* about the death in 1978 of Chuck Stevens, then twenty years old. He died as a consequence of a fraternity hazing incident at Alfred University in which he was locked in an automobile trunk after having been given large amounts of alcohol.[6] The students who inflicted this misery were not simply immune to his suffering, they enjoyed his suffering. They enjoyed having all the power with Chuck having none. They relished their total domination over a fellow human being. Like the Marquis de Sade, "they elevated cruelty to a major virtue."[7]

I don't know the identity of the students who took part in this grotesquely stupid tragedy. I do not even know their names. But I think I can tell you quite a lot about them. They were not very intelligent; if they had been they would not have engaged in such ludicrous nonsense. But neither were they stupid; after all they were the beneficiaries of a college education. They were average American boys who meant no harm and who, I imagine, must have been utterly devastated by the tragic outcome of their little prank. They certainly did not mean to do something evil, and least of all to commit murder. They just wanted to have some fun. And fun to them consisted of depriving a fellow student of all dignity, of all independence, of all self-esteem to the point of death. If the Mafia had committed the murder, I would not have mentioned it: the Mafia will murder. But these were normal, average boys, not very much different from our sons or grandsons, brothers or fathers when they were young. That is why I tell the story. For there, but for the grace of God, go I, we, they. The hazers enjoyed having absolute power over another human being and that power corrupted them absolutely. In miniature they acted out the stuff of which the concentration camps were made, particles of which permeate post–World War II society, producing abused children, battered women, maltreated prisoners, neglected inmates, all victims of absolute power.

"For thine is the kingdom and the power and the glory. . . ." I would like to think that these prayerful words mean that the power is not ours but derives from the source of all power we call God, and is to be used by us, as fiduciaries, not for our own purposes but to bring about the kingdom in glory.

15

Vanity and Validity

Vanity of vanities, saith the Preacher, vanity of vanities; all is vanity. What profit hath a man of all his labour which he taketh under the sun? . . . All things are full of labour; man cannot utter it. . . . The thing that hath been, it is that which shall be; and that which is done is that which shall be done: and there is no new thing under the sun.

Ecclesiastes 1:2–3, 8–9

ESTELLE: . . . *I've six big mirrors in my bedroom. There they are. I can see them. But they don't see me. They're reflecting the carpet, the settee, the window—how empty it is, a glass in which I'm absent! When I talked to people I always made sure there was one nearby in which I could see myself. I watched myself talking. And somehow it kept me alert, seeing myself as the others saw me. . . .*

Jean-Paul Sartre
No Exit

The book of Ecclesiastes is a worldly book. Generations of theologians have wondered what prompted the church fathers to include it in the "canon," the collection of inspired and inspiring writings that form the Bible as we know it today. For the worldly skepticism of Ecclesiastes is hardly inspiring. Its pessimistic cynicism, however intellectually sophisticated and beguiling, makes it rather a dead end of the spirit.

Its leitmotif is expressed in the opening verses: "Vanity of vanities, saith the Preacher, vanity of vanities, all is vanity."

Now, the noun *vanity* has as its corollary the adjective *vain*, and *vain*, according to the *Random House Dictionary*, has two meanings: (1) excessively concerned about one's own appearance, qualities, achievements; and (2) uneffectual, unsuccessful, futile, without real value, senseless.

It has occurred to me that the significance of Ecclesiastes may lie in the ambiguity of these two meanings and that its message may be found in equating them. For doesn't excessive preoccupation with oneself—vanity—make one futile and one's actions senseless—that is, vain? And doesn't the act of overcoming that vanity by focusing one's interest, one's abilities, one's love on one's fellow human beings instead of on oneself make one valid and one's actions meaningful? It would indeed transform us, in a very basic way, from self-oriented persons into other-oriented persons.

This transformation may be triggered by small events. A recent newsletter of Massachusetts General Hospital described a program that had been quietly developed on the pediatric wards for the benefit of young patients who have to be hospitalized for a long period of time. Many have working parents who can visit but rarely, and Mass. General, as a great medical center, has many child patients who come from far away, from other states, from other countries. Their parents cannot visit them, not even occasionally; there are no friends, no relatives whose visit can break the monotony and loneliness of hospital existence. They hurt, these children, they are sad. They do not want to eat.

The program developed for these children is the "Foster Grandparent Program." To become a foster grandparent one has to be more than sixty years old; one must have a limited income and plenty of time, energy, and love to share. It is not a volunteer program. The foster grandparent makes a commitment of twenty hours a week and in consideration thereof receives a weekly stipend, free lunch, and free transportation. Many a foster grandparent has health problems, but this does not prevent them from establishing an affectionate relationship, a bond of love, with the foster grandchild. And it works like magic: the children look forward to their foster grandparent's visit, to being read to, played with, to having their company at mealtime or even being fed by them; they recover from their depressed state, both physically and emotionally.

But there is an additional result, one neither intended nor expected: improvement in the health of the foster grandparents. Their blood pressure comes down; their sleep improves; their energy increases as they spend far more hours than agreed upon at their foster grandchild's bedside. The program triggers in both the foster grandchild and the foster grandparent the transformation from self- to other-orientation. Both turn from vanity—in the sense of preoccupation with self—to validity.

Other small causes can trigger similar transformations. A group of radiologists—so I was told—found marked differences in the tolerance of radiation treatment and the subsequent recovery among their older patients who were living alone, some single, most of them widowed. The differ-

ences were not—to their surprise—related to differences in the malignancy for which they were
treated. Patients with far less invasion of their
bodies by malignant cells did not seem to tolerate
the treatment better, recover earlier, or experience
fewer recurrences than the patients with more
invasion of their bodies. The source of this unexpected anomaly was found to be this: although all
patients were living alone, some had pets, a dog, a
cat, a parrot. *They* were the ones who—sometimes
against apparently great medical odds—made the
better recovery. They were less prone to the de-
pression and discouragement that often accom-
pany the radiation treatments. Nothing more than
having a pet triggered that life-giving transformation away from the self, toward the other, from the
vainness of life toward its validity.

What conclusion can we draw? Let me tell you a
story. A woman came to the great rabbi and said,
"I don't know what to do. At first I thought that to
be happy I had to be beautiful. I read beauty
magazines, spent an hour every day on my
makeup, and became beautiful, or so my friends
told me. But I wasn't happy. Then I decided that to
be happy I had to be rich. I went into business and
made a great deal of money. But I worked so hard
that my health began to fail. So I decided that
happiness lay in health. I joined a health club, gave
up smoking, began running three miles every day,
and now I am healthy. But I'm still not happy."
"Look, my child," the rabbi said, "in the window
there is glass and in the mirror there is glass. The
back of the glass in the mirror is covered with a
little silver. You cannot look through it. You can
see only yourself in it. When you seek beauty and
wealth and health only for yourself they act like the
silver on the glass of the mirror: they prevent you

from seeing others and enable you to see only yourself. The happiness you seek is not in the mirror. It is passing by your window." Indeed, in the mirror we see preoccupation with ourselves, vanity, vanity of vanities. And through our window we see life, warm, throbbing, real life; life which gives us the chance to establish relationships with our fellow human beings that reflect the ultimate mystery into which we are born, relationships of love and care and compassion.

We do not find any such relationship in the book of Ecclesiastes. Which brings me to the second reason why the church fathers may have included this so worldly book in the Bible. Ecclesiastes has a "no exit" quality, similar to that of the play *No Exit* by Sartre, which depicts the fate of three persons who cannot satisfy each other's emotional needs and are doomed to spend eternity together. In their hell there is neither change nor renewal, neither death nor resurrection.

Old civilizations have a tendency to develop their own "no exits." The French say: "The more things change, the more they remain the same." Many years ago at a business luncheon in Paris I was asked to formulate in a few words my view of the difference between the United States and France. I remember saying: "In France, as your saying goes, the more things change, the more they remain the same. In the United States, the more things change, the more they change."

Ecclesiastes says:

The thing that hath been, it is that which shall be; and that which is done is that which shall be done; and there is no new thing under the sun. (1:8–9)

But Jesus, according to John's Gospel, taught his disciples:

A new commandment I give unto you, That ye love one another; as I have loved you, that ye also love one another. By this shall all men know that ye are my disciples, if ye have love one to another. (13:34–35)

The "no exit" mood of Ecclesiastes, "and there is no new thing under the sun," contrasts with Jesus' proclamation: "A new commandment I give unto you."

And it may well be that the church fathers included the book of Ecclesiastes in the canon in order to create that contrast. For this is the essence of the Judeo-Christian message: we are not trapped; creation is not a gigantic practical joke. There is light that beckons, there is newness that calls, there are powers of love that care, powers of compassion and forgiveness that redeem. It is never too late, nor ever too early.

16

Therefore, Choose Life

And God said, Behold, I have given you every herb bearing seed, which is upon the face of all the earth, and every tree, in the which is the fruit of a tree yielding seed; to you it shall be for meat.

Genesis 1:29

And the Lord God commanded the man, saying, Of every tree in the garden thou mayest freely eat: but of the tree of the knowledge of good and evil, thou shalt not eat of it: for in the day that thou eatest thereof thou shalt surely die.

Genesis 2:16–17

Perhaps someday someone will explain how, on the level of man, Auschwitz was possible; but on the level of God it will forever remain the most disturbing of mysteries.

Elie Wiesel
The Death of My Father

"Since what we choose is what we are," says the hymn. I think the hymn is wrong. If I could have chosen what to be, I would be a very different person from the person I am. I would be a good skier and a good tennis player, both of which I am not. I would be a scholar and I would look more—what shall I say—glamorous, with waving hair, a lot of white teeth, and a dimple in my chin. But no, I must make do with the gifts I have.

If the hymn had declared: "Since what we *do* is what we are," I could have made my peace with it; yes, more than that, I would accept it as the characterization of a principal human function. For what counts in the end is what we *do* as a result of the conscious choice we make between alternatives. In this sense, you might even say that what we choose—among given alternatives—determines what we are.

It is the ability to choose among alternatives that makes us human. Many learned books have been written to explain the strange coexistence of two different biblical accounts of the creation of humans. The two stories probably stem from different sources later amalgamated in the book of Genesis. Still, how to explain that two different stories about the same event have, over the ages, maintained themselves side by side? I like to think that the explanation lies in the fact that the stories portray not the same but different events.

The first one, the creation of humans in God's image, "male and female created he them," took place on the same day and as part (albeit a climactic part) of the creation of the animals. It represents the creation of humans as the crown of the animal kingdom.

The second one, the creation of Adam out of the dust of the ground, and of Eve out of Adam's rib, in the Garden of Eden, represents the elevation of humankind out of, and to a position above, the animals. For to Adam and Eve a choice is given.

In the first story, God specifically states: "Behold, I have given you every herb bearing seed . . . and every tree . . . yielding seed; to you it shall be for food." In the second story, he makes an exception and thereby creates the elements for a choice: "Of every tree of the garden thou mayest freely eat, but of the tree of the knowledge of good and evil, thou shalt not eat of it." Dilemma. Will they or won't they? A tough choice.

One more observation: only after all this has happened does God proceed to create Eve out of Adam's rib. This means that God's warning, his prohibition to eat from that tree, preceded the creation of Eve. She had no knowledge of it, at least not from the horse's, that is from God's, mouth. Adam was the only one who could have told her about this prohibition. And Eve may have had her own thoughts about it: was it really true that God had forbidden them to eat from that tree, or had Adam thought up the story in order to keep *her* from eating, while *he*, at night, stealthily ate from the tree and thereby preserved his domination over her? Who is to say?

Anyway, they chose to eat. And since then, knowing the difference between good and evil, they have had to make choices, one after the other all day long, and sometimes well into the night.

Making choices presupposes free will. If the chooser has no free will, then the choice is ultimately made not by the chooser but by whomever withheld or usurped that free will from the chooser. Under a dictatorship the people still vote, i.e., they go to the polls to elect their leaders. Only when 99 percent of the people vote for the same candidate, who happens to be the person who is in office anyway, one need not be clairvoyant to conclude that the whole thing was a farce, a complicated way for the dictator to vote for himself.

The biblical tree story clearly presupposes that God had given his human creatures a free will.

Otherwise the story does not make sense. It would
be like the dictator voting for himself. The free will
theory, however, conflicts with the assumption
that God is omniscient. For if God is omniscient,
everything is predestined. And if everything is
predestined, there can be no free will; we would be
puppets acting out a predetermined script. To
attribute free will to humans, therefore, means to
deny omniscience to God.

The book of Genesis is based on this denial. That
is why, after finding out that Adam and Eve have
eaten from the tree, God exclaims: "What is this
that thou hast done?" and in the next chapter, after
finding out that Cain has slain Abel: "What hast
thou done?" Hardly the reaction of an omniscient
being who has known it all in advance.

This conflict between human free will and divine
omniscience has puzzled theologians and philoso-
phers from Augustine to Calvin into our own age.
In fact, the problem precedes Augustine: the Jewish soldier and historian Josephus who was born in
Jerusalem in the year A.D. 37 says of the Pharisees,
who had coped with the same problem, "that they
believed in the divine dispensation but also in the
freedom of human choice."[1] This is what Rabbi
Aqiba (ca. A.D. 50–ca. 135) expressed in the sen-
tence, "Everything is determined but freedom is
given."[2] They solved the problem by not regarding
it as a problem.

A modern explanation offered by the philosopher Hans Jonas suggests "that in making unlimited freedom possible for the human being, God
has taken a great risk, has made a wager. Therefore
it is for us to accept the challenge of attempting to
vindicate God's wager. In a sense he is betting on
us."[3] He does not want to know in advance what
people will do and he does not want to keep them

from doing to each other the terrible things they have been doing since the beginning of time.

I personally find this theory quite unacceptable. I cannot visualize a deity as frivolous as Mr. Jonas's wagering God. I don't think God plays games. However, that leaves the problem unresolved.

Meanwhile, let's face it. The number of our contemporaries who are interested in the conflict between God's omniscience and human free will has dwindled. But the old problem has been resurrected in a new shape. The question to what extent our freedom is limited by God's omniscience has been converted into the question to what extent our freedom is limited by genetic and psychological conditions. The hymn declaring "Since what we choose is what we are" predates our knowledge about these limitations. For it was written in 1903, twelve years before Sigmund Freud made his insights into the realm of the unconscious known to the world, and sixty-five years before Nobel Prize–winning Professor James D. Watson published his book *The Double Helix*, which popularized "one of the key discoveries of the century, the structure of DNA, the heredity molecule." The theological problem is converted into a biological and psychological problem.

A nephew of mine is colorblind. Colorblindness is a genetic disease that prevents him from becoming an aviator; it is a choice he does not have. Severe stuttering prevents one from opting for the ministry, and cerebral palsy from choosing to be a ballet dancer. If Hitler in his youth had not been the miserable painter he was, but a gifted, widely recognized one, he might never have chosen to become the Führer of his criminal movement.

A recent article in *Newsweek* magazine about homosexuality states:

The question of choice is crucial: is being
gay merely a "life-style" or a matter of
"sexual preference"? Is it a personality
disorder [*sic*]? Or is it some genetic fact, like
being left-handed? If gays choose to be gay,
then that choice—like any human choice—
may be properly subject to criticism and legal
strictures. If being gay is part of their very
nature, then society should accept them.[4]

I do not quote this passage for its wisdom because
I do not think it has any particular wisdom; I quote
it because it reflects so well the confusion that
continues to exist between freedom of choice and
predestination.

> *The fault, dear Brutus, is not in the stars*
> *But in ourselves that we are underlings.*[5]

Shakespeare put these words in Cassius's mouth,
though the Romans in reality were less "either/or"
minded. They held that the stars *inclinant non
cogunt*, freely translated, that the stars create ten-
dencies, not destinies, that they incline but do not
force people to do certain things.

Our generation, which witnessed the birth of
nuclear physics, has less reason than any preceding one to apply the "either/or" stricture to the
solution of problems. Remember Robert Oppenheimer's warning:

If we ask . . . whether the position of the
electron remains the same, we must say
"no"; if we ask whether the electron's
position changes with time, we must say
"no"; if we ask whether the electron is at
rest, we must say "no"; if we ask whether it
is in motion, we must say "no."[6]

All this spells the end of the Aristotelian "either/or" logic. Why then should we continue to expect an answer to the question whether God is omniscient or we have a free will? The truth may be a thousand times more mysterious than even the electron's position, the answer a thousand times more complicated; or possibly so simple that it is beyond our comprehension.

Meanwhile we know certain things from experience: in our lives we are confronted with a limited number of options, God-given options, not of our making. But we have freedom—maybe total freedom—to make choices between these options. This choice-making is of the essence of our lives.

Today humankind as a whole is confronted with the most dramatic choice since its beginnings, a choice that will determine whether or not it will live. What comes to mind are the words Moses addressed to the children of Israel, at the historic moment when they were about to cross the River Jordan into the land the Lord had promised to their fathers; when he proclaimed:

> I call heaven and earth to record this day
> against you, that I have set before you life
> and death, blessing and cursing: therefore
> choose life, that both thou and thy seed may
> live. (Deuteronomy 30:19)

They chose life. May we do likewise.

5

Searching for Truth

17

Believing in Believing

> Unto you therefore which believe he is pre-
> cious: but unto them which be disobedient, the
> stone which the builders disallowed, the same
> is made the head of the corner.
>
> 1 Peter 2:7

> To decide between belief or unbelief is of the
> utmost importance, for such a decision radi-
> cally alters one's conception of oneself. But for
> those who even before such a decision are
> living according to fidelity to understanding,
> the intention and dynamism of their life do not
> change. They have merely found themselves.
>
> Michael Novak
> *Belief and Unbelief*

Some of my best friends are unbelievers. They
have no interest in religion and regard any preoccupation with theology as an eccentric way of
wasting time. This often troubles me. It is not that
I am concerned about their souls. Nor do I believe
that in an afterlife—if there is such a thing—we
would be relegated to different places, I to a place
where religiously concerned people spend eternity, and they to a place reserved for those who
during their earthly life were indifferent to religion.
No, it is not that.

Their unbelief troubles me for other reasons.
First, it affects our relationship. For isn't it true that

friendship between human beings is based on shared experience, shared concerns, shared interests? Their indifference toward matters of religion, with which I happen to be deeply preoccupied, limits, therefore, the extent and the depth of our friendship. It creates a no-man's-land between us. And that pains me.

There is another reason why I feel troubled: some of my nonreligious friends are exemplary human beings: honest, intelligent—some are brilliant scientists—concerned about social questions, always eager to help when help is needed. They make me doubt the justification of my preoccupation with religion; *I* seem to need something *they* can do without. They are at peace with themselves and the world; not always, of course, but by and large and without any religious support or base or undergirding. Great! And I feel tempted to be envious of so much maturity; I am inclined to be jealous of their unbelief.

It has been said that, historically speaking, periods during which people believe are followed by periods during which people believe in believing, after which they fall easy prey to the secularization process and become unbelievers. But the opposite is also true: many unbelievers are attracted to religion, they believe in believing and often become believers. Sometimes the process is spread over several generations: the most convinced believers may be grandchildren of unbelievers, while many believers propagate unbelievers.

So, the mix changes but the three categories of believers, believers in believing, and unbelievers have existed side by side in the Western world since the Renaissance created alternatives to the church's medieval monopoly over the mind of all Christendom.

The post–World War II period exemplifies how the mix can change. The first twenty postwar years saw an enormous increase in religious interest. Membership increased, churches were built, Sunday schools burst at the seams. Then came the late sixties, during which a disenchantment set in that continued during the seventies, in both the Catholic and the mainline Protestant churches. Budget surpluses turned into deficits, more churches were closed than opened, the age of unbelief seemed at hand. But elsewhere in the country a mighty religious movement was coming of age. "Evangelical Christianity . . . emerged from its anticultural ghetto unto the mainstream of American life."[1] In August 1976, when the mainline churches were still in decline, "the Gallup Poll discovered that one person in three (34 percent) had been *born again*—that is had had a turning point in his or her life marked by a commitment to Jesus Christ. This figure works out at nearly 50 million American adults." Today mainstream evangelicalism has become a reality. "The poll found out that a very high proportion of twice born Christians believe either that the Bible is the actual word of God and is to be taken literally, word for word, or at least that the scriptures are the inspired word of God, although not everything in them should be taken literally."[2] It is frightening, at least from where I sit. But certainly it refutes the theory that the age of unbelief is at hand. And the more believers there are, the more important it becomes to make a distinction between "believing" and "believing in believing."

I am a believer in believing. I realize that there are those who no longer believe. They may have passed through the phase I am in, or they may have skipped that phase; they may have passed directly from being believers to being unbelievers.

They may have gone from orthodoxy directly to what they—sometimes proudly—call atheism and what I think should, in most cases, more appropriately be called agnosticism. Maybe I should address myself especially to them in making my case for "believing in believing."

Let me first point out that my argument is not based on the slogan President Eisenhower promoted: "The family that prays together stays together," which seems more a utilitarian sociological admonition than a religious one, or the exhortation "Attend the church of your choice," which seems to exclude as unacceptable the possibility that one has no church at all. My case for believing in believing rests on these considerations: humans are decision-making animals. Life forces us continuously to make conscious choices among various options. Each choice makes a difference to ourselves, to our environment, and to other human beings. What I do as the result of a conscious choice makes a difference.

I sit on a crowded beach. A crying child comes my way. She has lost her parents. It makes a difference whether I take that child by the hand and comfort her and assure her that together we will surely find Mommy and Daddy, or whether I do nothing, or possibly show irritation and say to the child: "Go away." It makes a difference.

The option I choose depends to a large extent on the blueprint of behavior according to which I try to live, the code that represents my beliefs. For the religious transaction consists of my relating my behavior, my thinking, my life, and the choices I make in that life to a blueprint, a plan I have consciously adopted, a code in which I believe and to which I have committed myself; or maybe I should say to which I have submitted myself.

There are in the world a number of different plans
and codes. In our culture the predominant one is
embedded in what is sometimes called the Judeo-
Christian tradition. Again, maybe I should express
this differently: our culture derives from the plan, the
code that is embedded in the Judeo-Christian tradition. As Tillich has put it, religion is the "meaning-
giving substance of culture."[3] The guide, the hand-
book to that plan is, of course, the Bible, that amaz-
ing composite of history and stories, parables and
myths. But history is predominant. Ours is a religion
that was acted out in history, that came into being
with the unfolding of history, the history of the
Jewish people that culminated in the life and death of
one Jew, whose name was Joshua or Jesus.

And all these things to which the Bible refers
happened, or originated, between 5,000 and 2,000
years ago. No wonder that the plan is not as clear
as if it had just come off the press. It is sometimes
veiled, enigmatic; there are contradictions; it suffers from mistranslations and interpolations; it has
to be read in terms of what is written in the lines
and between the lines. But in the end the basics are
clear, clear and compelling.

It is incredible, isn't it, that the terms in which
we see, in which we experience life—and that
includes all of us, regardless of whether we call
ourselves Christians or humanists, atheists or ag-
nostics—are those coined and formed and hal-
lowed in a faraway land at the dawn of civilization
by a small Semitic tribe that was on first view not
very different from other Semitic tribes, but that
was destined to open up the vistas, to formulate
the concepts, to create the scale of values that still
dominate our lives.

Incredible indeed. For what do we have in common with those people who thought that the earth

was flat and the center of the universe, who lived in tents and most of whom were illiterate? Nothing. Nothing except things like the ideas of freedom and justice and the sanctity of every individual human being; nothing except the ideals of love and compassion and the insights in the redemptive value of suffering and the grace of the forgiveness of sins.

It is the very fact that we have little else in common with the people of the Old Testament that gives the depth of perspective to the things we do have in common, these core values of life we inherited from them.

The Bible is not primarily a book of philosophy or theology, of ethics or anthropology—though it includes all of these—but a history book. The biblical people in both the Old and the New Testaments are—with some additions and subtractions—historical people who lived and loved and sinned and suffered and who were different from others only because all this took place within the framework of their ongoing dialogue with their God. I spoke of the difficulties resulting from the fact that this plan stems from long ago and far away; that it originated in an environment with which ours has little in common; that it has to be interpreted and cannot be taken literally, as so many evangelicals today maintain it should. Even if we were able to put together a theological, philosophical, ethical code, perfectly clearly expressed in modern language and suited to our present-day situation, it would only be an effort to replace a historically grown system that has the perspective of eternity with a synthetic system that would lack the breath of the spirit. It has been tried. It has failed.

Take the Nazi philosopher Alfred Rosenberg. He wrote a book, entitled *The Myth of the Twentieth Century*, which was meant to supply the Nazi movement with a substitute for the "Semitic" Bible. Even that book referred to the past in that it tried to revive the belief in the Germanic Woden saga with which the composer Wagner had reacquainted the German people a generation earlier. Many people still like to listen to Wagner's music. But where is Mr. Rosenberg, and where is his *Myth of the Twentieth Century*? And for that matter, where are Hitler's quasi-prophetic book *Mein Kampf* and Mao's *Little Red Book*?

I have used terms such as "depth of perspective," "perspective of eternity," "breath of the spirit" in describing the characteristics of the biblical link between us and that historical experience which the German theologians call *Heilsgeschichte*, history of salvation. It seems to me that the constant measuring of our daily lives against that history of salvation conditions us, trains us, teaches us to see our lives and the choices of which it consists in the light of the motivating force that is explicit in the history of salvation the Bible records.

Do I believe that this motivating force is God? Maybe one could say that. How do I visualize this force? I don't know; I can't imagine it (but I do know that one of the ten commandments counsels us not to make images of God). Do I really believe that the history of the Jewish people and the life and death of Joshua/Jesus and everything he is supposed to have said and done and taught have a uniquely special significance for the fate of the world? That it really is *Heilsgeschichte*? I'm not sure. But I do believe that the assumption that it is the history of salvation is a most effective working hypothesis. No, I can't say that I believe. It would be presumptuous and not truthful. But I find it helpful to act as if I believed. I may not believe, but I do believe in believing.

18

Once upon a Time

Christianity (like Judaism) is an historical religion because it holds that life is a story. We Westerners are a biographical people, and even our science does not shrink from attempting to discover the biography of the material universe. . . . Since the Enlightenment, we have gone about diligently trying to separate the true stories (that is, history and science) from the myths. We have seemed determined to ferret out the one true "plot" of the universe.

Tom F. Driver
Patterns of Grace

Nontheist and theist in our society need one another. The theist tells the stories in whose light the values by which even the nontheist lives are dramatically illuminated. The nontheist chastens with his skepticism the luxuriant proclivities of the theist for idolatry and dogmatism.

Three generations hence, our children's children will be poorer if either the symbols or the skepticism are lost. Each of us chooses how much of both he will labor to transmit.

Michael Novak
A Time to Build

When I was born, eight years after the death of Queen Victoria and seven years before Albert Einstein would baffle the world with the mathematical formulation of his theory of relativity, science and religion had, for more and more people, become mutually exclusive; it was either/or. My parents—as their parents before them—were proud of their liberal heritage, which included complete emancipation from religion. My sister and I were taught that religion was for the uneducated; while we were told never to show disrespect for religion because many people "still believed in it," we were assured that with the passage of time education would catch up with the believing remnant and that in the end the truths of science would replace the superstitions of religion.

My parents—as my mother told me later—were therefore alarmed when at the age of five, possibly under the influence of a Lutheran nurse who read to me from a children's Bible she had smuggled into the house, I expressed deep concern about humanity's sinfulness and need of salvation. At the age of twelve I asked to go to Confirmation class and my liberal parents obligingly registered me in the Bible course of Dominee (Dutch for "Reverend") Ferguson, a former Dutch Reformed missionary in New Guinea, then part of the Netherlands East Indies. One of my classmates, named Luke, was a grandson of the Dutch physicist Professor Johannes Diderick van der Waals, a winner of the Nobel Prize.

Dominee Ferguson began at the beginning, i.e., he began with the creation, which, he said, took place in the year 4004 b.c., thereby following in the footsteps of the Irish archbishop James Ussher, who in 1654 had established that date, I don't know on what ground, specifying further that it happened on October 23 at 9:00 a.m. Up went my hand: "But, Dominee, in school we were told that it took millions of years before it all evolved."

Dominee was visibly annoyed but not unprepared. "I discussed this question," he said, "the other day with Luke's grandfather. And you know what the Professor said? He said: 'Of course it took millions of years but if I want to know how it really happened, I look it up in the first chapter of Genesis.' "

When I came home I asked my parents to take me out of the Confirmation class, which as good liberals they did, I suppose without regret.

More than sixty years have passed and I have often wondered why this incident disturbed me as a child and why I remember it so clearly up to this day. One reason may be that the great physicist, contrary to my parents, had apparently succeeded in combining the way of science and the way of religion; that, to put it in present-day terminology, he had managed to be, at the same time, a creationist and an evolutionist. For I did not then, nor do I now, have any doubt that Dominee Ferguson spoke the truth when he told the class about his conversation with the great professor. At the same time I felt deceived for a reason which I came to understand only many years later. For the professor, who believed in the story of creation as we find it in Genesis, would, I am sure, have rejected any suggestion that it happened in the year 4004 B.C. And my suspicion is that Dominee had not mentioned that date to the professor. And that makes all the difference. For the dating of the event converts the story of Genesis into history. And as history it is untenable in the light of science, and would certainly not have been acceptable to Professor van der Waals.

As story, however, it supplements and interweaves with science. Indeed there was a beginning, ten—or is it fifteen or twenty—billion years ago. A beginning that took place, so to say, from one day to another. Indeed, everything was in place when the first humans made their appearance on the earth. And it is true that humanity lost its animalistic innocence by acquiring knowledge of the difference between good and evil; and that it became aware of time and, as a result, knows about life and death.

It is only during the last fifty years that science has evolved the theory that there was a beginning and that the universe is not eternal. It is on the strength of scientific evidence developed during the last fifty years that the big bang theory has replaced the so-called steady state theory, which holds that the universe had no beginning and is eternal. But the sage who, some three thousand years ago, formulated the thoughts we find in the book of Genesis, knew apparently at that time what science has established only today. Robert Jastrow alludes to this astonishing fact when he tells us, in connection with the big bang theory, about the scientist who has "scaled the mountains of ignorance; he is about to conquer the highest peak; as he pulls himself over the final rock, he is greeted by a band of theologians who have been sitting there for centuries."[1]

Neither science nor religion has anything to say about *why* all this got started. Aristotle invented the Prime Mover, an uncaused first cause. The Bible calls it God. Tillich speaks of the God behind God. All right, but what is there behind that God? I agree with Tom F. Driver's observation that "this is simply to transfer the problem."[2] Some scientists, so I am told, entertain the thought that the whole thing (I mean the *whole* thing, the whole expanding universe with its billions of galaxies, each with its billions of stars) started at random. All I can say about *that* is that I would at least suggest, in this case, that random be spelled with a capital R. The difference is essential. It determines whether we derive meaning from the universe or have to bring meaning to it, whether meaning is revealed to us or created by us.

I want to revert to the dating of the act of creation by Archbishop Ussher. When Ruth and I recently spent some time in New York, we had lunch at a place called Old Denmark. On the wall were painted historical scenes from Danish history with explanatory texts, one of which read as follows:

> Once upon a time, a thousand years ago,
> there was a King, etc. etc.

Something bothered me about these words. Suddenly I realized what it was: the words "Once upon a time" stand at the beginning of a story, a timeless story. The words "a thousand years ago" date the story and by dating it convert it into history. The timeless is changed into the time-bound.

The great physicist J. Robert Oppenheimer said:

> These two ways of thinking, the way of time
> and history and the way of eternity and of
> timelessness, are both part of man's effort to
> comprehend the world in which he lives.
> Neither is comprehended in the other nor
> reducible to it. They are as we have learned
> to say in physics, complementary views,
> each supplementing the other, neither
> telling the whole story.[3]

When our grandson Benjamin was five, he declared, "You can always tell when a story isn't true, because if it begins with 'once upon a time' or if it ends with 'happily ever after' and you thought it was real then you were wrong." Astute little boy, Benjamin. But what he did not yet realize was that these unreal stories are often better conveyors of truth than historical facts.

Judaism and Christianity are historical religions. They are rooted in history. The Bible speaks of things that really happened. Not only of such things—the creation, for instance, is, at least in my opinion, not one of them—but to a large extent of such things. How then can we justify imputing a nonliteral story-character to the Bible?

I would like to submit two possible answers to that question which, I think, in the end, merge into one.

The first answer is given by Gerhard von Rad in his book on Old Testament theology. He points to the fact that a great part of even the historical tradition of Israel has to be regarded as poetry. "Historical poetry," he says,

> was the form in which Israel, like other
> peoples, made sure of historical facts, that
> is, of their location and their significance.
> In those times poetry was, as a rule, the one
> possible form for expressing special basic
> insights . . . poetry alone enabled a people
> to express experiences met with in the
> course of their history in such a way as to
> make the past become absolutely present.[4]

What von Rad says here, I think, is that poetry, or story, was the form in which history was encapsulated in order to be preserved as an ever-present reality.

The second answer is suggested by Frederick Turner in his book *Beyond Geography:*

> The more we come to know of history,
> the more it reveals itself to be symbolic,
> as the discrete events, artifacts and
> personages tend to lose something of
> their individualities and to become
> increasingly representative.[5]

What he seems to say is that history, the good old-fashioned history of things that really happened, has a propensity to adopt symbolic significance; that by shedding the tangible, factual details and historical particulars it adopts a symbolic quality and becomes story—story that transcends history. Von Rad and Turner, it seems to me, are speaking about the same thing.

Several summers ago we had as our guests two young physicists and their wives who came to see us at the suggestion of one of our daughters, whose husband teaches chemistry at Cornell University. They had interesting things to say about their careers. The physicists were involved in research on the behavior of atomic particles in an ultra-cold environment, the kind of environment created for the first time in the 1920s by the Dutch physicist Kammerlingh Onnes, another winner of the Nobel Prize. With the use of liquid helium he succeeded in reaching temperatures close to absolute zero. Strange things happen at these ultra-low temperatures at which the atomic turbulence that exists at higher temperatures is eliminated.

I asked the physicists to explain. I paraphrase what one of them said: "When the thermodynamic turbulence is eliminated, other strange forces can be observed that regulate the behavior of the particles. For instance, if you have an electron here and another one there, this electron here behaves as if it knew what that electron there is doing."

"Now you are telling me a story," I said. "An 'as if' story." "Yes," he conceded, "but stories are the means by which one can think about these things and talk about them and explain them to others. In the end you may get to an equation but that equation, in a way, is only shorthand for the story."

"What you are telling me," I said, "is that scientists speak in parables." They agreed. "What happens," I asked, "if a scientist forgets that he speaks in parables and begins to believe that the parable is literally true? What happens if the scientist one day disregards the 'as if' element and proclaims that that electron does not behave *as if* it knew what the other electron is doing but that it *actually knows* what the other electron is doing?"

The scientists looked perplexed at such absurdity. They politely inquired how I had arrived at it. "Because," I said, "that is what is happening in religion all the time; the story is taken literally, the parable is presented as being 'really true.' That is why in Europe the churches are empty and why in this country more and more churches are becoming the scene of mass infantilism. This is what Paul Tillich warned against when he said that 'the first step toward the non-religion of the Western world was made by religion itself. When it defended its great symbols not as symbols but as literal stories it had already lost the battle.'[6] Since Tillich wrote that, literalism has been embraced by tens of millions in this country."

Nobody spoke. We were all lost in thought. After some time I broke the silence: "It seems to me," I said, "that the *story* may well be the common denominator of science and religion. Only, scientists know that the story is a story that points beyond itself to truth, and religion too often falls victim to the temptation to proclaim that the story *is* the truth. That is why, in our days, science flourishes and religion is in trouble."

Following Tillich, who warned us never to say of something that it is "only a symbol" because the symbol, in his words, "points beyond itself,"[7] I believe that we may be making a grave mistake when we say, "Oh, that's just a story." Because, in the end, the tale, the story, the myth are the means by which we capture reality and come to terms with it. This is why Tom Driver is correct when he says that so often "stories are felt to be mysterious, even sacred, and are so often associated with religious experience. To 'get' a story is a kind of revelation."[8] It is in this spirit that the late eighteenth-century German poet Novalis wrote: "The history of Christ is just as much story as it is history. And altogether only that history is history which can also be story."[9]

I am a story person. I feel as Elie Wiesel did when he answered the question "Why did God create man?" with the words, "Because he loves stories."

In my book *The Mask of Religion* I wrote:

> We . . . are in danger of failing our
> heritage . . . by assuming that this heritage
> claims to represent the truth of religion
> when in reality it represents the story of that
> truth, the metaphor about that truth. That
> metaphor demonstrates in history what is
> beyond history. It speaks to us in terms we
> know about things we do not know. It uses
> words for things that cannot be expressed
> in words, concepts for things that are
> inconceivable. It addresses the truth by
> suggesting it and pointing to it, by invoking
> it and implying it. Yet this metaphor is not
> that truth and should never be confused
> with it.[10]

I am in good company. Robert McAfee Brown, professor emeritus of theology and ethics at the Pacific School of Religion in Berkeley, California, in redefining the nature of the theological task he has set himself for the remainder of his life, and the methodology with which he hopes to fulfill that task, writes:

> For me, the methodological ingredient of this endeavor is *story*. In claiming this I seek not to embrace a "fad" but to recover a lost emphasis. Our faith, after all, did not initially come to us as "theology," and particularly not as "systematic theology." It came as story. Tell me about God: "Well, once upon a time there was a garden . . ." Tell me about Jesus: "Once upon a time there was a boy in a little town in Palestine called Nazareth . . ." Tell me about salvation: "Well, when that same boy grew up, he loved people so much that the rulers began to get frightened of him, and do you know what they did? . . ." Tell me about the church: "Well, there were a great many people who were attracted to Jesus and started working together: Mary and Priscilla and Catherine of Siena and Martin Luther and Martin Luther King and John (several Johns: John Calvin, John Knox, John XXIII) and Gustavo and Mother Teresa, and do you know what they did? . . ."
> Out of such stories the systems begin to grow, with results we know only too well: stories about a garden become cosmological arguments; stories about Jesus become treatises on the two natures; stories about salvation become substitutionary doctrines of atonement; stories about the church become by-laws of male-dominated hierarchies. . . .

In losing the story we have lost both the power and the glory. We have committed the unpardonable sin of transforming exciting stories into dull systems. We have spawned system after system: Augustinian, Anselmian, Thomistic, Calvinistic, Lutheran, Reformed, orthodox, liberal, neo-orthodox, neo-liberal. Historically they were very different; today they share in common an inability to grab us where we are and say, "Listen! This is important!"[11]

We must recover the story if we are to recover a faith for our day. Not any story will do. What I— and, I think, Robert McAfee Brown—have in mind is the story that has a metaphoric quality, meta-phoric in the literal sense of the Greek *metapherein*, which means "to carry from one place to another," that is, a story by which one feels carried away, carried away from the seen to the unseen, from the imaginable to the unimaginable. Conversely, this kind of story may be seen as the projection of the unimaginable into the world of the imaginable, as the medium through which the sacred enters into the world of the profane, as an epiphany of the spirit.

If you accept this and train yourself to be sensitive to stories that yield spiritual insights, you will find that not a day passes without a spirit-enriching experience. It may come to you when you are at work or when you follow Walt Whitman's admonition "loaf and invite your soul." It may come to you when you are listening to music or when you look at a painting. Life situations may take on a story character and thereby open up perspectives of the spirit. And of course literature will; in fact, poetry sometimes offers a shortcut in the most unexpected ways from the profane to the spiritual. As in the poem by Bradford Smith, written in the 1960s shortly before he died. He called it "Wonder."

The sky's on fire! The sky's on fire!
Would it burn if I touched it with my hand?
The boy child stands with head thrown up,
His toes curled to the sand.

Would I bump my head if I went up high,
If I went up high as a bird?
If my head touched the sky would I hurt and cry?
Would God be mad if he heard?

Why is water wet? Does the brook run all night
Or does God turn it off while I'm sleeping?
Does the brook ask questions like me when it talks?
Is that why it's running and leaping?

Why do roses have thorns. Does God love a thorn
As much as he loves a rose?
We've loaf and fishes for dinner tonight.
See how our lily grows.

Is the sun really hot? Does it cook the sky?
Can birds go to sleep? Can water get dry?
Were things like this when you were a boy?
Can I have this piece of wood as a toy?

Something like this were the words he said,
Warm with wonder of life at the dawning;
With the wonder of life and no thought of death—
This carpenter's son of Nazareth.[12]

Greater poems have been written but none more poignant. The story element in it is overwhelming.

Jesus, the master storyteller, "teaches hardly anything without a parable," as Tom Driver observes. "If we learn lightly to tell stories and gently to play with them in our mind, then we may know how to read and hear them."[13]

Let us follow his advice and tell each other stories; not in order to escape from the reality of life, but in order to come to grips with it and have it more abundantly. Let us use our capacity to conceptualize the mysterious reality into which we are born and to tell each other the stories about that reality which together form our religious tradition. But we must at all times remember that these stories are *not* the truth, but tell us something *about* the truth and that the question, therefore, should not be "Is that really so?" but "Does it say something to us about the way things really are?"

I think it was Elie Wiesel who said: "The way things really are goes beyond our comprehension, but let me tell you a story. . . ."

19

What Became of Hell?

> *The theist . . . believes that the stories told in his community of faith—of genesis, exodus, promised land; of expectation, contradiction, death and resurrection—illuminate the truth of human life. The theist finds human experience symbolic as well as secular; significant as well as pragmatic. He believes history to be a conversation, a dialogue; responsibility is response to a hidden lover. The stories are not merely stories; their point is real.*
>
> Michael Novak
> *A Time to Build*

> *If the church wants to clear itself of the anti-Jewish trends built into its teaching a few marginal correctives will not do. It must examine the very center of its proclamation and reinterpret the meaning of the gospel for our times. . . . In his* Voice of Illness *Aarne Siirala tells us that his visit to the death camps in eastern Europe after the war overwhelmed him with shock and revealed to him that something was gravely sick at the very heart of our spiritual tradition.*
>
> Gregory Baum, Introduction to
> Rosemary Ruether,
> *Faith and Fratricide*

Religious liberals have abolished hell. In consequence they have done away with a central tenet of

139

orthodox Christian belief: that in the end of time
Jesus will return in glory to judge the living and the
dead. In this judgment the righteous will be re-
warded with eternal heavenly bliss and the sinners
punished with eternal suffering in hell. As if this
were not enough, there was a generally held belief,
expressed by Gregory the Great, who occupied the
papal throne from the year 590 to 604, that "the
bliss of the saved in heaven would be incomplete
unless they would gaze across the abyss and behold the sinners tormented in hellfire." I wonder
how Pope Gregory would have felt about Hitler's
concentration camps. This is not a frivolous question. Many have observed a certain parallel between the camps and hell in the Christian tradition. According to George Steiner:

> The camp embodie[d], often down to
> minutiae, the images and chronicles of Hell
> in European art and thought from the
> twelfth to the eighteenth centuries. It is
> these representations which gave to the
> deranged horrors of Belsen a kind of
> "expected logic." . . . The concentration
> and death camps of the twentieth century,
> wherever they exist, under whatever
> régime . . . are the transference of Hell from
> below the earth to its surface. They are the
> deliberate enactment of a long, precise
> imagining.[1]

This, I think, illustrates what Gregory Baum
means when he refers to "the illness operative at
the very heart of our spiritual tradition." This
illness can be traced throughout the history of the
Christian world. It did not express itself only in the
church's anti-Judaism, for, as Samuel Sandmel
observes: "The cruelties wrought on Jews in the

Rhineland in the First Crusade [1096–99] were at least matched by the horror inflicted in the Fourth Crusade [1202–4] on the Byzantine Christians in the pillaging and destruction of Constantinople."[2]

Or take the genocidal persecutions of the Albigensian heretics of southern France in the thirteenth century; they led to the institution of the Inquisition, which raised havoc among the alleged enemies of Christ within the church over a period of five hundred years. Or think of the cruelties committed in Palestine by the crusaders over a period of several hundred years. Or of the strange witch burnings, a true form of persecution of women by men, which took place all across Europe over a three-hundred-year span, and in this country expressed itself in the happenings in Salem Village. These burnings, which began in the fifteenth century, were sanctioned and encouraged by several popes. In fact the manual for the cult of witch burning was written by two Dominican monks.

How do we explain this long history of cruelties committed by or in the name of the church? I don't know, but I believe that it is somehow related to the peculiar Christian theology with its Last Judgment, its heaven and its hell.

If this is so, then the elimination of this three-layered universe, of an earth sandwiched between heaven and hell, by our enlightened spiritual ancestors may have gone a long way to curing that "illness operative at the heart of our spiritual tradition." However, in abolishing heaven and hell, they destroyed at the same time Western humanity's solid framework of morality: the good were to be saved, and the bad were to be condemned. Infantile? Maybe. But solid. And with the infantilism the solidity has gone out of Western life. I know, I know: the good deed carries its own reward and the crime is punished by the criminal's bad conscience. But that is not at all the way it is in real life. I don't think that Hitler and his cohorts suffered from a bad conscience. In fact, in 1943 the notorious Heinrich Himmler, in addressing a body of SS lieutenant-generals about the annihilation of the Jews, declared: "Most of you know what it means to see a hundred corpses lie side by side, or five hundred, or a thousand. To have stuck this out and to have kept our integrity, this . . . in our history is an unwritten . . . page of glory. . . ."[3] So much for the criminal's bad conscience. What comes to mind is Mitya's desperate exclamation in Dostoyevsky's *The Brothers Karamazov*: "Without God . . . anything is allowed."[4] For if there is no God, there is no Last Judgment, no accountability, no punishment; nothing is prohibited. And then again, it may not be that simple.

Many years ago I saw a television skit I shall never forget: a man sat behind a table and in front of him there was a long queue of people. The man behind the table addressed the person at the head of the line and said in a somewhat bored but otherwise businesslike voice: "Of course you know that you are dead. All you have to do now is to go through the entrance on your right behind me marked 'heaven' or through the left one marked 'hell.' " The dead man looked incredulous. "You mean that I, uh, am to choose whether I want to go to heaven or to hell?" "That's right," said the man behind the table." "But," said the dead man, "is there no judgment? Does it not count how I have lived, the good things I have done and the bad things?" The man behind the table showed the first signs of impatience. "Look, man," he said, "I cannot spend the whole day on you. People are dying, the queue is lengthening. Make up your mind." The dead man by now was in a panic. "But I have sinned, I have done horrible things, I want to come clean, I want to confess, I want to be judged, I want to be forgiven. . . ." The man behind the table no longer took the trouble to hide his impatience. "I am not interested in your sins and nobody else around here is. Make up your mind, that's all I'm asking of you." The dead man looked horrified. He hid his face in his hands to think; then he stepped forward past the table and disappeared through the entrance on his left marked "hell."

In the end we want to be accountable; in the end we want to confess; in the end we want to be judged and ultimately to be forgiven, for all of us have done things we shouldn't have done and all of us have omitted doing things we should have done. At the same time we are the heirs of those enlightened minds who abolished heaven and hell, who did away with the Last Judgment, thereby creating a vacuum we have never been able to fill. Still, while most of us do not believe in heaven or hell, we behave as if we did believe in them. While it has become story to us, it is still a story that tells us something about reality. For it is *not* true that everything is allowed, it is *not* true that it makes no difference what we do or do not do. It makes a difference; it makes *all* the difference.

Back to Dostoyevsky's Mitya, who warned that if God did not exist, everything was allowed. Can we possibly turn it around and say: As not everything is allowed, God does exist? And some judgment or at least some accountability does exist?

And now it seems that we have come full circle: first I blamed the concept of the Last Judgment for the illness at the heart of our spiritual tradition.

And now I say that in the end there must be some judgment, because not everything is allowed. It sounds contradictory, but it isn't. For in anticipating the Last Judgment, human beings have too often played God and condemned their fellow human beings to hell on earth. They acted as if their fellow human beings were accountable to *them*, weighed and found wanting. The accountability *I* recognize is not the accountability of *others* to me, but it is *my* accountability to—ah—to whom? To God? To my superego? To myself? I would rather say, with Michael Novak, that my accountability, my responsibility is "response to a hidden lover"[5] whose redemptive love is both judgment and forgiveness.

20

Risk-Taking

And Gideon said unto God, If thou wilt save Israel by mine hand, as thou hast said, behold, I will put a fleece of wool in the floor; and if the dew be on the fleece only, and it be dry upon all the earth beside, then shall I know that thou wilt save Israel by mine hand, as thou hast said. And it was so: for he rose up early on the morrow, and thrust the fleece together, and wringed the dew out of the fleece, a bowl full of water.

Judges 6:36–38

She was a vagabond agitator who lived a hundred years. At the age of thirty-six, she was Mary Harris Jones, the wife of a union member and the mother of four young children. A year later, the Memphis yellow fever epidemic of 1867 had left her a childless widow. She moved to Chicago and opened a dressmaker's shop, which, along with her home, was destroyed four years later in the Chicago fire. Annealed by personal tragedy, she devoted her energies to unionism and improving the life of working people, especially those who worked in the mines. . . . The woman who became known as "The Miner's Angel" was regularly jailed and lived where she was needed, often sleeping on the floor of a worker's shack with her purse as a pillow. She was adamant about her motivation: "Get it right, I'm not a humanitarian. I'm a hell raiser."

Andrea Fleck Clardy
Mother Jones

I am the owner of an Atmos clock. You know, one of those clocks that has no moving parts and runs on the changes in the atmospheric pressure. I received it as a gift a long time ago. For many years it adorned my office in New York and when I retired, it stayed behind because it was too frail for casual transportation. Recently a former colleague of mine offered to have the clock cleaned, reset, professionally packed, and shipped to me at Cape Cod. "Do you think that is safe?" I asked him. "If you have any qualms, why don't you have it insured?" he replied. So I got an estimate and insured the clock for the estimated value. It gave me a sense of great relief. The clock was insured; I had eliminated all risk; I was safe; nothing untoward could happen. This elation, so much out of proportion with the frivolous event that had caused it, made me think about the nature of insurance. I arrived at two conclusions. One, that the most important values in life, the things that really matter, cannot be insured. I cannot insure the happiness of my marriage, the normalcy and the virtue of my children and of their offspring. I cannot buy insurance against disaster.

To give you an example: Ruth and I were married in Amsterdam in 1939. Within a year after our marriage our little boy had died. One month after his death, the Nazis invaded Holland. And, again within a year, the day came when we left our apartment, each carrying a small suitcase, never to return, leaving behind all our belongings, our books and photographs and all the lovely, irreplaceable things that had belonged to our parents and to theirs. We had become refugees. And while that was our salvation, it carried its own risks and its own pain.

Conclusion number two: the terms *health insurance, life insurance, fire insurance* are unintentionally misleading. The insurance does not protect your health or your life, it does not prevent your property from being burned to ashes. It only means that you will be reimbursed for the expenses of sickness, that you get back part of the monetary value of your burned possessions, that your heirs will get some money when you die. It is not insurance *of* your life but insurance *on* your life. Mind you, I am not criticizing the concept of insurance. I believe in insurance, as exemplified by my insuring the Atmos clock. What I'm saying is that insurance has its limits, that the real values in life, the things life is all about, are not insurable. We have to take the risk. And it may well be that it is this very risk that makes those uninsurable things so movingly precious. For how happy would a happy marriage be if its happiness were guaranteed? How valuable freedom if it were inviolable? How dear would life itself be if it were not at all times threatened by the risk and ultimate certainty of death?

There is a difference—though the line is not always easy to draw—between risks that are inherent in life, risks that exist by the nature of things, and risks that I consciously decide to run because the rewards outweigh the chance of loss. Of course one can make a mistake in judgment, as the eminent British scientist Lord Rothschild pointed out in a recent lecture when he quoted the Chinese proverb: "The couple who go to bed early to save candles end up with twins."

Mother Jones's identity exemplifies the two types of risk: her children die, her business goes up in flames, built-in risks, not of her choosing. But then, with incredible faith, she decided to take all the risks that went with her efforts to improve the life of working people, especially those who worked in the mines. You don't become known as

"The Miner's Angel" if you are afraid of taking risks.

There are known and unknown risks. The inhabitants of the town of Bhopal in India had no idea of the risk they were running by living in the shadow of a Union Carbide plant until the day disaster struck. Similarly, while we know the statistics about air traffic accidents, we have only the vaguest notion of the frequency of near misses, the accidents avoided by the tiniest of margins in the crowded airspace above our airports. And what about the ultimate risk, the risk of nuclear war? Never before has humankind felt threatened by a risk so inconceivable, so total, that it lacks the terms in which to express its horror.

The word *risk* is not found in the Bible. I have been wondering why. The answer, I believe, is that risk implies an element of chance and, to the ancients, chance as a concept did not exist. What appeared to be chance was God's will to them. If, during a thunderstorm, I seek protection under a tree, I know that I run a risk of lightning striking that tree. It is a matter of chance. To the ancients, it was a matter of God's will. And as long as God made his ultimate will clear to the risk-taker, the risk was no longer a risk. It was eliminated by faith.

When God tells Moses to go to his people and prepare them for the exodus, Moses answers: "But . . . they will not believe me or hearken unto my voice." In order to increase Moses' faith, God enables him to do two miracles: to transform his rod into a snake and to change the snake back into a rod. That is the first miracle, and the second is that he can make his hand leprous and restore it to health. And God adds that if the people will not believe him in spite of the two miracles, and will not listen to him, then all he has to do is take some water from the Nile, pour it upon the dry land and the water will be turned into blood. When we go on our way in our car, we carry a spare tire with us. Moses went on his way taking a spare miracle with him. To bolster his faith.

Gideon is willing to take the risk God wants him to take, but only if God performs a few miracles to increase Gideon's faith to the point that it eliminates the risk. And God obliges: the fleece is wet with dew, so wet "that he wrung enough dew from the fleece to fill a bowl of water," while the ground around the fleece was dry. And the next day the fleece is dry while the ground around it is wet with dew.

Both in the case of Gideon and in the case of Moses, I have spoken of their faith. Maybe I should not have said *faith* but rather *confidence*. For what God does is to convince Moses and Gideon that he will arrange things through them and bring about a happy ending. God strengthens their confidence in their ability to fulfill the task he assigns to them. He persuades them that they run no risk in doing what he wants them to do: there will be a happy ending; nothing *will* go wrong.

Faith, I believe, is something else. Faith is the deep conviction that, whatever happens, even if there is no happy but a very unhappy ending, nothing *can* go wrong. This faith is exemplified in the following story, taken from the chronicle of one Salomon Ibn Verga, dated from the year 1550:

I heard from old emigrants from Spain that a ship full of refugees was ravaged by pestilence. The captain put them all ashore in uninhabited land. Many starved to death; only a few mustered the strength to start out

in search of an inhabited area. One of them
[by the name of Jossel] was accompanied by
his wife and two little sons. The woman,
unaccustomed to walking long distances,
grew weak and died. [Jossel] carried the
children until he fell down, exhausted.
When he came to, he found that his two
sons had died. In his grief he arose and
said: "Lord of the worlds. You do much to
make me give up my faith. Know then that
in spite of the heavenly powers I shall
remain a Jew. Whatever calamity you have
visited or will visit upon me will be of no
avail." Then he took some dust and grass,
covered his dead children with it and went
his way in search of an inhabited place.[1]

The spirit of this story lives on in testimonies of
survivors from Hitler's death camps who were no
less or no more religious because of what the Nazis
did to them, and whose faith in God was not
undermined in the least. It did not occur to them to
associate the calamity they were experiencing with
God, to blame or cease believing in him, because
he did not come to their aid. You see, Jossel's faith,
and that of these particular death camp survivors,
was total. Their faith was unconditional. It did not
depend on happy endings. For them the concept of
risk did not count. It was swallowed up in their
total faith. While confidence is *because of*, faith is *in
spite of*.

Most of us are people of little faith. Risks loom
large in our lives. Risks against which there is no
insurance, risks against which we cannot protect
ourselves.

Somebody once said, "A ship is safe in a harbor,
but that is not what a ship is for." The same applies
to us. We are here to take risks. I am speaking not

only of the built-in risks I mentioned earlier, the known and unknown risks built into our existence by the nature of things; we cannot escape them even if we wanted to. I speak also of the risks we accept knowingly and voluntarily, risks we run in order to live our lives the way we feel we should live them, to pursue the goals we have set for ourselves, the ideas to which we devote ourselves. Foremost among them is the risk we take when we love. We cannot live without loving others, and each time we love someone we take a risk, the risk of being rejected. We cannot live without trusting others, and each time we trust somebody we take a risk by making ourselves vulnerable to the misuse of that trust. And all these risks, the built-in ones and the chosen ones, we take, confident of a happy ending. But they do not always end happily, as all of us know only too well. It is *then* that faith should take over, faith in the ultimate goodness of creation, faith in the goodness of the unhappy ending, faith in God.

6

Coming Home

21

The God Who Suffers

And the Lord said unto Satan, Behold, all that
he has is in thy power; only upon himself put
not forth thine hand.

Job 1:12

On a rusty iron throne,
Past the furthest star of space,
I saw Satan sit alone,
Old and haggard was his face;
For his work was done, and he
Rested in eternity.

And to him from out the sun
Came his father and his friend,
Saying, —Now the work is
    done
Enmity is at an end—
And He guided Satan to
Paradises that He knew.

Gabriel, without a frown;
Uriel, without a spear;
Raphael, came singing down,
Welcoming their ancient peer;
And they seated him beside
One who had been crucified.

James Stephens
"The Fullness of Time"

During the days following the earthquake that
struck Mexico in 1985, the press reported the fate

of an eleven-year-old boy who was buried under the rubble of the building where he had been living with his grandfather. The old man somehow escaped and implored the nearest rescue crew to save his grandson. They started digging and after two days established contact with the boy by responding to his knocking on the walls of his cave. They worked feverishly though with great care lest they put the stones into motion and endanger the boy's precarious shelter. After one more day the knocks became weaker and the next day ceased altogether. The men gave up. The place where the ruins had sheltered the little boy had become his grave.

The thought of him and his fate has remained with me. I have been wondering why. My generation, having lived through two world wars, many local conflicts, and the Holocaust, is accustomed to learning about dead by the millions. One million Jewish children perished in the Holocaust, but, as somebody once said, one dead child is a tragedy, a million is statistics. Apart from that, there is a difference between the death of the Mexican boy in the earthquake and that of the Jewish children in the Holocaust. The latter were the victims of human depravity. The Mexican boy was the victim of—ah, of what? Of nature? Of fate? Or—dare I say it—of God? Certainly no human being can be blamed for the little boy's suffering and death; in fact, human beings tried to save him—albeit in vain.

And then, in the end, there may be no difference between the two. Sure, we can blame human depravity for the Holocaust, but where was God when it all happened? God, the all-good, the all-powerful? I have no answer to that question. Some think they do. Their answer is that it was all the doing of Satan, the mythical angel who led an unsuccessful revolt against God and was, with his followers, cast out of heaven. Satan, who in Judaism, Christianity, and Islam represents the principle of evil conceived as a person, that is, the Devil. He has gone by numerous other names: Beelzebub, the Evil One, Lucifer, the Prince of Darkness. The last two names pose an interesting question, for Lucifer means literally "carrier of light," a curious name for the Prince of Darkness. Be that as it may, Satan, though cast out of heaven, maintained an apparently cordial relationship with God, as exemplified by the book of Job:

> Now there was a day when the sons of God came to present themselves before the Lord, and Satan came also among them. (1:6)

There follows a conversation that may be paraphrased as follows:

> *The Lord:* What have you been up to?
> *Satan:* I've been looking for trouble.

And then the Lord says to Satan:

> Hast thou considered my servant Job . . . a perfect and upright man, one that feareth God, and escheweth evil? (1:8)

After some more discussion, the Lord reaches an understanding with Satan concerning Job, which he summarizes as follows:

> Behold, all that he hath is in thy power; only upon himself put not forth thine hand. (1:12)

And so the scene is set for Job's misery. Are God and Satan playing games? If so, why? What induces or forces God to traffic with the devil, to "trade with the enemy" to the detriment of human beings?

The questions are unanswerable. We are confronted with a mystery. Maybe the Job story is meant to serve the purpose of maintaining the monotheistic concept of an all-good, all-powerful God in a universe in which the just and the innocent suffer. For if the plight of Job and of the little Mexican boy and the millions who died in the Holocaust and the wars and of all who perished and are daily perishing in hospitals, traffic accidents, and by their own hands were laid at the feet of God, this would compromise his all-goodness. If, on the other hand, we assume the existence of powers of evil uncontrolled by God, whom one can blame for Job's plight and that of the others who suffer, this would compromise God's all-powerfulness.

Here's where Satan comes in: we can blame him for the evil in this world without affecting our monotheistic stance. For Satan is not a god of evil opposing a god of good. In fact he is not a god at all. He is nothing but a rejected, rebellious angel, a servant of the good God, who until the fullness of time is allowed to stick around as God's fall guy.

This reasoning—or something close to it—seems to satisfy most orthodox minds, be they Catholic, Protestant, or Jewish. It does not satisfy me. I cannot absolve God of at least some responsibility for the evil Satan wreaks in the world. After all, Satan—in the symbolic language I have been using all along—is his servant. For me, therefore, the mystery persists. My question remains unanswered.

An even more painful question is raised by Dr. Robert McAfee Brown:

> The deliberate murder of six million Jews by those who were shaped by an ostensibly Christian culture, makes forever impossible some of our previous theological assertions about a) the inherent goodness of human nature, b) a universe in which all things work together for good, c) any equation between justice and virtue, or d) just about anything else. A pall is forever cast over complacent or triumphant orthodoxies.
> There is little of past Christian theology, let us face it, that is "credible in the presence of burning children."[1]

"A pall is forever cast over complacent or triumphant orthodoxies," orthodox Christian or liberal Christian or humanist orthodoxies. We cannot go on as if nothing happened. We cannot do business as usual lest we drift further and further away from reality.

Sometimes I fear that this is exactly what some of us are doing. For one of our liberal-religious orthodoxies is the orthodoxy of optimism. We are the heirs to an optimistic worldview rooted in the Renaissance, which came to fruition at the time of the Enlightenment and merged in the nineteenth century with America's boundless expectations. This optimism leaves little room for the tragic and the dismal, for failure and despair. We cherish the heritage that abolished hell and eternal damnation and fostered social improvement and civil rights. But we have to admit that this perspective does not do justice to the world of Auschwitz and Hiroshima.

I want to carry Dr. McAfee Brown's question one step further by asking not only whether Christian theology, but whether an all-good, all-powerful God remains credible in the presence of burning children. Logically speaking the answer is no. The evil invalidates either God's all-powerfulness or God's all-goodness.

In Archibald MacLeish's play *J.B.* this dilemma is presented in Nickles's—that is, the devil's—song about Job:

> *I heard upon his dry dung heap*
> *That man cry out who cannot sleep:*
> *If God is God he is not good,*
> *If God is good he is not God;*
> *Take the even, take the odd.*[2]

No doubt those who witnessed the evil of the Holocaust and did nothing to avert it are guilty. I know I am among them with millions of others. The Allied authorities who knew what was going on in the camps and always advanced reasons not to bomb the railroad tracks leading to them are guilty. The Germans who committed the crime are guilty in the first place. But what about God? And God's guilt? This is not a rhetorical question. Nor do I raise it exclusively with regard to the Holocaust.

In an earlier chapter I mentioned a tradition in Judaism that holds that even God cannot forgive one human being's sins committed against another; only the victim can. The rabbinical teachings claim that "sins committed against God are expiated on the Day of Atonement. Sins committed against one's neighbors are not expiated on the Day of Atonement until they are first forgiven by the victim."[3] In our day Emmanuel Levinas has written: "A sin committed against a human being can be forgiven only by the victim; God cannot do it. In honor of his own morality and of human dignity God is here powerless."[4]

In the Lord's prayer we pray: "and forgive us our trespasses as we forgive those who trespass against us. . . ." *Us*, mind you, not "against anybody." For we can only forgive the sins committed against us—not those committed against others.

Emotionally I have extended this thought to include God. I cannot forgive him for what he allows to happen to others. Only the victims can forgive him. I am therefore doomed to go through life with a feeling of resentment against God. I have a hunch that I am not the only one who feels that way.

In the small town where we live, a while ago, a young man drove his girl home from a party at about one o'clock in the morning. The young man leaned over to pick up a tape that had fallen from his tapedeck. He did not know that during the day the road had been resurfaced and that a pile of sand had been left at the end of the resurfaced stretch. Just when he leaned over, his front wheels hit the pile of sand. He lost control of his steering wheel and the car turned over. The young girl was dead. There was no alcohol involved, no drugs, nothing. But she was dead, three weeks before her eighteenth birthday. The boy was not guilty in any moral or legal or other sense. But he will have to live with the haunting memory of that night, he will have to carry that burden throughout his life. And he is twenty-two years old. Can one help feeling resentment, resentment against God?

Let me restate the theology that underlies this resentment.

We know that we cannot quarrel with God about things that happen to us personally. We know that we have to accept our fate as did Job of old: "Blessed be the name of the Lord." As did Jesus: "Thy will be done." The acceptance of our fate with all its suffering and pain is a religious act. But it is different with the fate of others. I can find their fate unacceptable. My refusal to make my peace with their fate is also a religious act, especially if I try to avert or to mitigate their fate. But that is not always possible. And if nobody does anything about it and the victims are victimized, then we cannot help saying, "O God, why didn't you do something, why didn't you stop that abomination?" And we are resentful. Could that also be a religious act? I know that this may sound unreal and irrelevant to unbelievers, and scandalous to believers. But I cannot help feeling this way.

In his play of that name, John Updike's dying President James Buchanan confesses what could be our own confession: "I am not troubled by the sins of men, who are feeble; I am troubled by the sins of God, who is mighty."[5]

How does God justify himself in inflicting suffering on the just? In the book of Job, he does it in a way I have always found hard to accept; he does it by ridicule and intimidation:

> Where wast thou when I laid the
> foundations of the earth? declare, if thou
> hast understanding. Who hath laid the
> measures thereof, if thou knowest? . . .
> Whereupon are the foundations thereof
> fastened? or who laid the corner stone
> thereof; when the morning stars sang
> together, and all the sons of God shouted
> for joy? Or who shut up the sea with doors,
> when it brake forth, as if it had issued out of

the womb? . . . Hast thou commanded the
morning since thy days . . . ? Hast thou
entered into the treasures of the snow, or
hast thou seen the treasures of the hail . . . ?
Canst thou bind the sweet influences of
Pleiades, or loose the bands of Orion?
(38:4–31)

And so it goes on verse after mighty verse, page
after poetic page. Job is duly shattered and answers the Lord:

I know that thou canst do every thing. . . .
I abhor myself, and repent in dust and
ashes. (42:2, 6)

However, God's answer to Job does not mention
that the whole thing started with Satan daring the
Lord and the Lord suggesting that Satan test Job,
his upright, loyal servant, possibly in order to keep
Satan's attention away from the less virtuous who
might indeed have fallen victim to Satan's seduc-
tive temptations. If this is so, God would have
sacrificed his virtuous servant in order to save the
sinful ones. Sounds familiar, doesn't it? But it
would cast doubt on God's all-powerfulness vis-à-
vis Satan, it would mean that there are limits to
what even God can do.

If there is an answer to the question why God
permits the just and innocent to suffer, it is based
on a strain in the Christian tradition that makes
suffering desirable. For, did not God, in the person
of his son, suffer on earth? Suffering therefore
brought the believer closer to God. As Thomas à
Kempis wrote in the middle of the fifteenth century:

O Lord, cheerfully will I suffer for Thy sake,
whatever Thou shalt will to come upon me.

From Thy hand I am willing to receive
indifferently good and evil, sweet and bitter,
joy and sorrow, and for all that befalleth me,
to give Thee thanks.[6]

A very Christian confession. And then again
don't we hear in this text the echo of the words of
Job who, sitting in dust and ashes, admonished his
wife:

shall we receive good at the hand of God,
and shall we not receive evil? (2:10)

And

The Lord gave and the Lord hath taken
away; blessed be the name of the Lord.
(1:21)

Still, Thomas à Kempis's beliefs contained one
concept that was unknown to Job: the concept of
God having suffered. I think that Rabbi Harold
Kushner is correct when he observes that "Christianity introduced the world to the idea of a God
who suffers, alongside the image of a God who
creates and commands." That indeed was a great
Christian innovation, a new dimension that Christianity added to Judaism. For as Kushner writes:

Postbiblical Judaism also spoke of a God
who suffers, a God who is made homeless
and goes into exile along with his exiled
people, a God who weeps when he sees
what some of his children are doing to
others of his children.[7]

And so we are confronted once again with the
mystery of the all-powerful who permits the just

and the innocent to suffer, but who also, as a cosufferer, joins them in their suffering, who comforts them and gives them strength to accept their fate and by accepting it, to overcome it. For only acceptance of life in all its manifestations of suffering and pain, will lead to more life. As the acceptance of death contains the elements of the Resurrection.

22

Mourning

A recent Sunday's *New York Times Magazine* brought an article entitled "A Lesson in Tragedy."[1] It was the story of the friendship between Astronaut Captain Ellison Onizuka, one of the seven crew members of the space shuttle *Challenger*, which perished on January 25, 1986, and a fourteen-year-old boy, Derek Simonds. It started just by chance. Seven years ago Derek's stepfather, a journalist, met Captain Onizuka and asked him for an autograph for his space-obsessed stepson. Captain Onizuka sat down and wrote the seven-year-old boy a long letter full of space jargon and science-fiction terms.

The letter was hand delivered to Derek by his stepfather with the assurance that it was from a real astronaut. "Oh, *sure*," said Derek. He did not believe it until a huge manila envelope from NASA arrived two weeks later with shuttle materials and photographs. One of the photographs was an eight-by-ten print of Ellison Onizuka, autographed "To Derek with best wishes. Good luck with the Xeron Space Patrol."

As the years passed and shuttle after shuttle was launched, Derek and his stepfather would read through the crew lists to see if Ellison Onizuka was on board. Finally in January 1984 they saw that he was listed as a mission specialist on the first fully classified Defense Department shuttle flight. In October 1985, out of the blue, an invitation came inviting Derek and his stepfather to attend the 1986 launch, the launch that was to meet with disaster and to turn the ecstatic expectations of this four-teen-year-old and of the entire nation into black despair. Derek saw the space vehicle with his friend inside explode into nothingness. "It just went up," he said afterwards, "and all of a sudden. . . . It's so hard to face the fact that Colonel Onizuka and the others were actually in there, that the shuttle actually exploded. The reality of it is so hard."

The article describes how the boy and his step-father helped each other during the first few weeks of grief and mourning. One day Derek said: "One thing I don't think is right, is that America as a whole has such a short lived memory of things. It's a couple of days of intense mourning and then it's forgotten, you know? People just don't care any-more. That attitude of 'it's not happening to me so forget it.' It's so selfish."

It is this observation of Derek's that made me think about the nature of mourning. I came to the conclusion that only if we feel that what is happening is happening to *us* can we mourn. If we do not feel directly involved, we can sympathize with the mourners, we can feel sorry for them, we may regret that the person who died did die but we cannot mourn, because, indeed, it is not happening to us. I think that as a nation we can and do mourn the astronauts because what happened to them happened not only to their parents and spouses and children and friends, but also to us as a nation because they were *our* astronauts and their failure, brought about through no fault of theirs, was *our* failure.

Ruth receives regularly the bulletin of the Kurn Hattin School in Vermont, a residential school for children of families with limited means who are under severe psychological stress. In it a boy from the fifth grade writes:

It is too bad that the space shuttle crew gave their lives for us. I know what Valentine's Day is all about. My Valentine's wish is that they will always be remembered.

This fifth-grader's thoughts are similar to Derek's: that they gave their lives for us is a valid basis for mourning and we must always remember them.

We mourn not only for what *was* and no longer *is*, we also mourn for what might have been and will not be. Mourning the death of children, of young people, of men and women at the height of their lives. Mourning the astronauts' deaths.

In the Kurn Hattin bulletin I mentioned earlier, a second-grade girl is quoted as having asked her teacher why God had let such an awful thing happen. The teacher asked the child what the minister had said about that in church on Sunday. The child paused and said, "He said God doesn't make bad things happen to people. *His* heart was broken, too." The little girl had asked her teacher the most important theological question of our tortured century. The little girl's minister exonerates God: "his heart was broken too." He is a good minister. I, for one, like to believe in God the comforter, the cosufferer, who, with a broken heart, mourns with us and ultimately is the source of new life, the God of the Resurrection.

I realize that by saying these things I get further and further away from objective reality. For it is not up to us to judge. It is not up to us to decide what God could, should, or might have done. Because it has not been given to us to understand. I would rather forget about the theology underlying these tragedies and look upon them as the mysteries they are. For to us apply the words of the psalmist:

> They know not, neither will they
> understand; they walk on in darkness: all
> foundations of the earth are out of course.
> (82:5)

I would rather let the theological question "How does one explain?" be and concentrate on the question "What does one do?"

David Rankin addresses this question in his description of an accident.

> The mother waited for her child at the bus
> stop. The bus arrived on time, deposing
> the passengers on the other side of the
> highway. The eight-year-old boy broke from
> the group and began running across the four
> lanes of concrete. The blue Cadillac crushed
> him like a plastic doll.

> In the living room that day:
> You tell her to speak to God.
> You tell her to eat and to sleep.
> You tell her to look to the future.

You tell her to walk in the cool air.
You tell her to bear the pain and sorrow.
You tell her to think of the other children.

But your face is wet with tears; and your
heart is gripped by grief; and your mind is
lost in darkness; and your soul plunges
wildly into the desolation of the valley—
where all words are symbols of absurdity.

Yes, there will be another day. But today
there is nothing to do but share the tragedy.
There is nothing to do but cry!

Is there a difference between the death of the
little boy in David Rankin's story and the astronauts? Of course there is: the little boy's death—as
far as we in our human limitation can judge—was
a senseless death. The astronauts' death—even if it
should turn out to have been avoidable—was not a
senseless death. They died in the service of a
cause: humanity's conquest of space. Does this
mean that the families of the astronauts have less
reason to mourn than the family of the little boy?
Sorrow cannot be measured. It is as total in the one
case as in the other. Yes, there will be another day.
But when disaster strikes there is nothing to do but
share the tragedy and cry and thus comfort and
strengthen the bereft.

Two days after the *Challenger* perished, we received the news that the son of one of our closest
friends, who lives in Holland, had died. He was a
radiant, lovable, gifted human being, a star in his
profession, happily married with three small children. One who had a love affair with life. He had
died just like that. His heart gave out without
warning. I felt the need to speak to his father, my

old friend, and say some comforting words to him. But when I got him on the phone and had hardly begun to speak, I started crying and was unable to resume the conversation. I felt embarrassed: nothing like it had ever happened to me. But Ruth said that my tears probably comforted him more than anything I could have said. And I knew she was right. Indeed, as David Rankin put it: "there is nothing to do but share the tragedy. There is nothing to do but cry!"

I remember as a young boy being taken by my mother to a funeral of some relative. Many people were crying. My mother said to me: "They all cry for their own dead." Indeed, we all mourn some loved one. We are all in mourning, a mourning that in some measure fills the emptiness left by death.

23

The Times of Our Lives

> *To every thing there is a season, and a time to*
> *every purpose under the heaven: a time to be*
> *born, and a time to die. . . .*
>
> Ecclesiastes 3:1–2
>
> *What matters dies, but matter lives?*
> *What never lives can't die;*
> *That only dies which lives—death is life's*
> *   badge,*
> *And life is death's. So I salute them all—sky*
> *House, trees, lawn, marble, clod. Stay then*
> *   and let me by.*
>
> Bradford Smith
> *Dear Gift of Life*

Ruth loves the spring. Therefore it pleases her when I say on the day after Christmas: "Today is the first day of spring." I say it every year, and every year it works. It works because it is true: after Christmas the days begin to lengthen.

Of course, it is not *quite* true. The shortest day of the year, the winter solstice, is December twenty-first. That really is the date after which the days begin to lengthen. If we see in Christmas the old pagan celebration of the winter solstice—onto which the Christian celebration of Jesus' birth was grafted—the renewal of the light represented by the lengthening of the days, then we should observe Christmas on December twenty-first. If, on the other hand—as is the case in our culture—we celebrate at Christmas the birth of the Christ, Christmas should be observed on January first since his birth is the event with which our calendar begins.

Is December twenty-fifth a compromise between the two dates? I don't know. But I do know that the days between Christmas and New Year's Eve have a strange quality of timelessness and suspense. They are like a no-man's-land between an end and a beginning. During these days time behaves as if it did not quite know what to do with itself.

Still, it passes. Time passes continuously. We may, individually, experience its speed as irregular. We all know what it means when somebody says that "seconds seemed an eternity" or conversely that "time flies." But, whether experienced as fast or slow, time flows irresistably, relentlessly, impassively. And our lives run out. One more Christmas is gone and in a few days another year will be gone. How many more Christmases, how many more years will be given to each of us? We don't know.

On the late afternoon of November twenty-seventh, the day after Thanksgiving a few years ago, I entered the emergency room of Massachusetts General Hospital. The tests started immediately and went on until close to midnight. The next day it was decided that, in order to keep functioning, my heart needed a pacemaker. In view of the oncoming weekend, the insertion was scheduled for the first of December, a three-day wait. Like most people, I felt anxious about the prospect of an imminent operation. I derived no comfort from the length of the waiting period. I knew that time was ticking away, that soon it would be one day before the operation, one night, a few hours, a few minutes. "Are you ready, Mr. Fleck?" No, the three days of grace did not comfort me. But what if the delay had been not three days but three years? Ah, that would have been a different matter. I am sure my anxiety level would have been much lower, maybe zero, or at least close to zero. For, as we say, in three years a lot can happen. Which, coming from the lips of a young person, may mean, "They may develop a medication that makes the operation unnecessary." Coming from the lips of an elderly person, they represent a euphemism for saying, "By that time I may be dead." For death is the only exit from life's waiting room. That is why those who believe in an afterlife speak of "life eternal," that is, life liberated from time's finiteness. But in this life we are time-bound, our days are numbered. In this realization lies the essence of life. Says the psalmist:

> The days of our years are threescore years
> and ten; and if by reason of strength they be
> fourscore years, yet is their strength labour
> and sorrow; for it is soon cut off, and we fly
> away. . . . So teach us to number our days,
> that we may apply our hearts unto wisdom.
> (90:10, 12)

Our days are numbered. Their number is unknown to us. There's the rub. The rub and maybe the blessing. Though I am not sure.

These days I have very childish conversations with myself, not worthy of my age, my stage in life, the wisdom one is supposed to have gained with time and whatnot. To be honest, the conversations are not so much with myself as with God. What I am saying is something like this: "Dear God, I am now seventy-eight years old and still quite healthy and able to do many of the things I have always liked to do, to read, to write, to sail, to be with people, to enjoy the company of my friends, the best of whom is my wife Ruth. I don't know, God, what the hereafter looks like but I sometimes have doubts, grave doubts (I don't want to sound disrespectful and if I do, I sincerely apologize) whether it can hold a candle to some of the things life on earth has to offer, in spite of all the earthly tragedy and suffering, the bomb and hunger and the misery in hospitals and prisons, in old people's homes and mental institutions and among those outside who cannot cope. And some time ago there was the Nazi scandal which we escaped by a hair's breadth, for which we give daily thanks. I assume that in the hereafter we shall all be free from the misery that affects all people some times and some people all the time. And that would be good. But what about the B-Minor Mass and *Figaro* and Beethoven's symphonies, and sailing on Pleasant Bay, and picking raspberries with the grandchildren in the summer? And what about seeing the sun rise over Nauset and set over the bay at Rock Harbor?

I have sat at the bedside of friends and prayed with them that death might come and set them free from their pain and anguish. I know that I myself some time, sooner or later, may be in that final agony, praying for death to deliver me.

But that still is no answer to my qualms about letting go of those things that have graced this earthly life. And if I have to sit on a cloud for the rest of my life (I beg your pardon—for the rest of my afterlife) I would at least want to have Ruth sit beside me. Ruth who listens so well and laughs so generously and who has that great gift of feeling deeply and saying funny things—and *not* some stiff-shirt angel.

By now my one-sided conversation with God is no longer serious, and I know it. Meanwhile, however, I have received the inkling of an answer:

the hereafter is so different, so unbelievably different from anything we can imagine, that we have no choice but to accept it on faith. Faith that it will be good and that it will in some way encompass all the wonderful things we have experienced in this life, which may turn out to have been but glimpses of the things to come.

Ruth's brother who died a while ago of cancer was told by his doctor two and a half years before his death that he would have some two years to live. He told us, when he came close to the end, that they had been the happiest years of his life. He was a fine sailor. During the first of his two remaining summers, he still sailed; during the last summer, when he was no longer able to sail, he sat in his beach chair, overlooking the bay, enjoying the coming and going of the sailboats. "The winds were never so gentle, the colors never so bright, the sails never so white." That is how he described it. He must have known that it was his last summer. He saw the temporary things of this world in the light of eternity. He lived on the threshold of time. From where he was, everything became meaningful. For life derives its meaning from death. And lends that meaning to time.

Says the preacher: "For everything there is a season and a time for every matter under heaven." First he mentions, "a time to be born and a time to die." And then comes the litany of times and seasons, including

> a time to plant, and a time to pluck up that
> which is planted . . . a time to break down,
> and a time to build up; a time to weep, and
> a time to laugh; a time to mourn, and a time
> to dance; . . . a time to get, and a time to
> lose; a time to keep, and a time to cast

away; . . . a time to keep silence, and a time
to speak. . . . (Ecclesiastes 3:2–7)

It has occurred to me that the good life is led by
those who are sensitive and responsive to the
rhythm of these times of our life, and who behave
according to the demands they make upon us and
the opportunities they offer us. Shaw quipped that
"youth is wasted on the young." Perhaps, but it
belongs to them and not to the old.

There is a time to be born and a time to die. If this
were not so, if life continued forever, we would not
be human. Our humanity depends upon our finiteness. This is not a new thought. It is as old as the
story of Adam's and Eve's expulsion from paradise
as we find it in the book of Genesis. Many people
believe that in the story Adam and Eve were expelled
because they ate from the tree of knowledge. Wrong.
There was a second, often forgotten, tree in that
story, the tree of life. It was lest they also eat from
that second tree, the tree of life, that they were
banned from the place. In the words of Genesis:

And the Lord God said, Behold the man is
become as one of us, to know good and evil:
and now, lest he put forth his hand, and take
also from the tree of life, and eat, and live for
ever: Therefore the Lord God sent him forth
from the garden of Eden. . . . (3:22–23)

Right there, at the beginning, we find embedded in
the paradise story the truth, that without death we
would not be human, that human life exists by the
grace of human death. To the degree that we
accept the inevitability of death do we realize the
wonder of life.

That is what Ruth's brother did when he looked

at the sailboats during that last summer of his life. He saw them both for the last time and for the first. He was happier than ever before. Because he saw life from the threshold of death. For he was dying. But aren't we all?

Most people don't want to be reminded of it.

The other day a parishioner said reproachfully to me: "You preach too much about death. People want to hear about life." She may have been right. In our society people don't like to hear about death, they don't want to be reminded of it. The idea that life and death are two sides of the same coin is abhorrent to them.

It has not always been that way. In his autobiography, entitled *Growing Up*, Russell Baker describes how, around the turn of the century, death was experienced in the village of Morrisonville in Virginia, where he grew up:

> Morrisonville had not developed the modern disgust with death. It was not treated as an obscenity to be confined in hospitals and "funeral homes." In Morrisonville death was a common part of life. It came for the young as relentlessly as it came for the old. To die antiseptically in a hospital was almost unknown. In Morrisonville death still made housecalls. It stopped by the bedside, sat down on the couch right by the parlor window, walked up to people in the field in broad daylight, surprised them at a bend in the stairway when they were on their way to bed. . . .[1]

I am sure that the topic of death was not avoided in those days, that it was freely talked about without self-consciousness. I can imagine that one developed a certain familiarity with it, in those days, in spite of the awe it must have inspired then, as it does now. I believe that privately we still develop some of that familiarity. I know this, as do most people my age. For me, as for them, the preoccupation with death is a daily event.

I found it, therefore, very appropriate when I was asked the other day to preach on the theme "If I die tomorrow," because in a way, and to a degree, I try to live every day as if I were going to die tomorrow. For isn't that exactly what is going to happen? I mean not necessarily today's tomorrow, but certainly one of these days' tomorrow.

Recently a young friend asked me whether I was afraid to die. I said no. I am not afraid to die, but sometimes I am afraid about how I'll get there from here. For on the way many suffer illness, anxiety and pain, loneliness and the loss of independence, until Death comes to them as a friend and takes them into his everlasting arms. Besides, I sometimes feel that dying, that is leaving this world, is not my responsibility but that of the Power that brought me into this world. And I trust that Power.

Our oldest daughter, at age five, gave this answer to her four-year-old sister who had anxiously inquired about dying: "It is nothing to be afraid of. It is just as if you were invited somewhere, and it is getting late and you go to the hostess and you say, 'Thank you for the wonderful party, I really enjoyed myself, but now it is time to go home.' "

I have never heard it better expressed. So if I were told that I would die tomorrow, I hope that I would feel as our daughter's little guest at the party. And as Bradford Smith felt when he wrote, eleven days before his death:

> *It takes no courage for dying,*
> *But rather a quiet mind.*[2]

What would I do with that last day? I would like to talk on the phone with my children and grand-children, and write a few short notes to some old friends. I would like, with Ruth, to listen to some recordings from the Saint Matthew Passion, maybe read aloud a few beloved passages from some cherished book. But, essentially, I would not want the day to be different from other days, except that I would ask Ruth to cancel her appointments so we could spend the whole day together. And if in summer—health and weather permitting—go for a short sail; if in winter, for a short walk. And spend some of the time together in silence.

After dinner, I think I might feel as Dylan Thomas felt in his story *A Child's Christmas in Wales*. After a day of snowballing with his friends, helping extinguish a fire at a neighbor's house, receiving and giving presents, seeing his uncles with exaggerated gestures smoke big cigars, singing Christmas songs with an uncle playing the fiddle and a cousin singing "Cherry Ripe," when everybody was laughing, he went to bed.

> Looking through my bedroom window,
> out into the moonlight and the unending
> smoke-colored snow, I could see the lights
> in the windows of all the other houses on
> our hill and hear the music rising from them
> up the long, steadily falling night. I turned
> the gas down, I got into bed. I said some
> words to the close and holy darkness, and
> then I slept.[3]

24

Dear Gift of Life

*There is none like unto the God of Jeshurun,
who rideth upon the heaven in thy help, and in
his excellency on the sky. The eternal God is
thy refuge, and underneath are the everlasting
arms.*

Deuteronomy 33:26–27

*As I watch'd the ploughman ploughing,
Or the sower sowing in the fields, or the
    harvester harvesting,
I saw life there too, O life and death, your
    analogies;
(Life, life is the tillage, and Death is the
    harvest according.)*

Walt Whitman
"As I Watch'd the Ploughman Ploughing"

In the first chapter I tell a story my mother used to read to me before I could read for myself. It was the story of a gnome who lived in a dark forest. As you may remember, he was not a happy gnome. There was another gnome in that forest, one who did lead a happy and contented life until he was awakened early one morning by the smell of smoke and the weird, frightening, crackling noise of burning trees: the forest was on fire. The little gnome was seized by a panic and began to run away from the fire. On the road he passed a number of fire engines from the surrounding villages speeding toward the fire from which he was fleeing. It did not reassure him; if anything it increased his panic. He ran until he came to a sign, reading: "You are approaching the end of the world." But he was so intent on running that he did not see the sign. He passed a second sign, reading: "This is the end of the world." He did not see it either; he just kept running, running, running . . . and then he fell off the edge of the world.

Of course, I knew that it was just a story, a folk tale. But somehow to me, at the age of three or four or five, whatever it was, it had an ominous ring of truth: in my mind's eye I saw the rim that constituted the end of the world and the little man stepping into nothingness . . . falling, falling into bottomless, endless space. Nor was I impervious to the paradox of that little man who kept running to save his life and thereby lost it.

The Dutch poet P. N. van Eyck tells us the story of a Persian nobleman's servant who met with a similar fate. One day the servant, working in his master's rose garden, finds himself suddenly confronted with the person of Death. Death makes a gesture toward the servant. The servant panics, runs to his master, tells him about the gruesome encounter, and begs for his fastest horse so he may escape to the great city of Ispahan, the best hiding place he can think of. The master gives his permission and the servant gallops away.

Later in the day the master, curious about his servant's story, goes to the rose garden and is pleased to find Death still there. "Why did you frighten my servant?" he asks. Death answers: "I did not want to frighten your servant. My gesture was one of surprise."

Surprise that I found here the man
I am to fetch tonight in Ispahan.[1]

Both the gnome and the servant ran for their lives—into the arms of death!

Many of us are afraid of death, if only because we do not know what dying means, we do not know what happens to us after death. The unknown is always frightening. It has occurred to me that a similar fear must exist among the unborn souls, wherever they may be, if there are such at all. If so, these unborn souls are probably afraid of being born, which, I imagine, is as inevitable for them as dying is for us. They are afraid because being born spells the end of their preincarnate existence, just as death spells an end to our incarnate existence. "If there is life after birth," they might say to each other, "and mind you that is *very* doubtful, we can't know a thing about it. And the unknown is always frightening. No wonder," they conclude, "that we are afraid of being born."

When we are young, death seems remote. We do not give it much thought. It is something that happens to others, mostly to old people. When we approach the age of fifty, we seem to turn our attention from the cradle to the grave. We no longer see our lives in terms of what has happened to us since we were born, but in terms of what we may expect, or hope, or bring about to happen before we die; we live no longer *from* a beginning but *toward* an end.

Many things may mitigate our fear of death. During the first year of the Nazi occupation when we were still in Holland, we befriended an old Viennese Jewish couple. Three years earlier they had escaped from Nazi-occupied Vienna to Amsterdam where they found themselves once again

under Nazi domination. In those days there was a
kind of black market in poison pills that were
guaranteed to kill in a moment. Our elderly
friends—like many others—had bought two pills,
one for each of them, which they carried with them
wherever they went. They had only one fear, the
fear that they had been fooled and that the pills
might turn out to be sham. They—as many in
those days—were more afraid of life than of death.
To them, as to many others, death was the net
under the trapeze of the world's perversity, God's
everlasting arms of which the book of Deuteronomy speaks. In a world of persecution, death was
their friend, death was their refuge. I for one shall
never forget that the fear of life can outweigh the
fear of death, that death can be the saving grace
from life's terror.

All of us have relatives or acquaintances who,
finding life unbearable, sought and found refuge in
death's saving embrace. Underneath are the everlasting arms. With part of our being all of us, in
varying degrees, look forward to this refuge. At
times we may feel like the man who had his
tombstone in the ancient cemetery of Lübeck in
Germany inscribed with these words: "When thou
callest me, Lord Christ, I will arise but first let me
rest awhile for I am very weary."

To use a Freudian term, we all have a death
wish. Any love affair with life implies a love affair
with death for life derives its meaning from death.
A deathless world would be hell. And still we are
afraid of death. We shouldn't be.

Most religions present elaborate beliefs about life
after death which, like so many security blankets,
enable the believers to face death with equanimity,
if not with joyous anticipation. Ours does not.
Ours presents the mystery and seems to say to us:

"There, solve it, and if you cannot solve it, live with it."

Thoreau, when asked to speak on the afterlife, is supposed to have disqualified himself with the words: "One life at a time."[2] I respectfully disagree with him. True, death is a mystery, we do not know what dying means, we have no information about life after death, if there is such. But it is exactly this lack of knowledge, this total ignorance about the meaning of dying, combined with the certainty of it, that we should think, ponder, meditate about while we are still alive.

The young are excused from this exercise unless a life-threatening illness or the death of a close friend, or any other specific experience, makes them realize early in life that in the end they too have to die. To others this realization comes late in life. I remember that, only a few years ago, after my hospitalization for heart trouble, I said to Ruth: "Now I really begin to believe that I, too, will die one day." Of course, it was meant facetiously—but not entirely.

"We usually refuse to face [death] for ourselves until something forces us to," wrote Bradford Smith in the final months of his life.

> Then, strangely, the response is not fear any longer, but acceptance, even contentment. . . . You can relax, take time to drink in all that is beautiful, listen to all the music your soul longs for . . . read the books you have longed to go back to, let nature sink in through every pore, spend more time with those you love, and ease the string to your bow so that living loses its tenseness but not its joy.[3]

You remember Dylan Thomas's poem:

Do not go gentle into that good night,
Old age should burn and rave at close of day;
Rage, rage against the dying of the light.[4]

He wrote it for his dying father. He was thirty-eight years old. As usual, the advice given by the young to the old was the wrong advice.

Bradford Smith offered a deeper insight when he wrote:

Once you have faced the fact that you
yourself are mortal, today's dawn, since it
may be the last, comes with all the force and
newness of the first, and so eternity is bent
within the arc of personal experience. So
time, though it threatens the great erasure,
is itself erased.[5]

I believe he is right. His is the story of one who meets Death in a rose garden and is *not* afraid. He does *not* try to escape but enters into a dialogue with Death and that dialogue illumines life. Yes, it becomes clear that only such a dialogue enables one to fathom the deepest reaches of life.

Not everybody meets Death in a rose garden. In our cruel age many have met Death in concentration camps, on battlefields, in the slums of the third world's overcrowded, swollen cities, and also, with great suffering, throughout our country's hospitals, prisons, old people's homes, and mental institutions. But these miseries only accentuate Death's grace.

Walt Whitman wrote:

I do not think Life provides for all and for
  Time and Space,
but I believe Heavenly Death provides for all.[6]

And again:

> *Come lovely and soothing death,*
> *Undulate around the world, serenely arriving,*
>   *arriving,*
> *In the day, in the night, to all, to each*
> *Sooner or later, delicate death.*[7]

He, too, made his peace with death and in doing so he made his peace with life. With life in this world. This brings us face to face with the ultimate pain. For if it is true that we make our peace with life by making our peace with death, then we pay with our lives for making peace with life. What remains is the sadness of separation. Separation from the beloved, from children, grandchildren, friends, from home and garden, from books and music, from sunrises and the reflection of the full moon on the bay. Or is there possibly no separation but rather a merging in which all becomes one? We don't know. We'll soon find out.

Meanwhile, we give thanks for the dear gift of life, with all its pain and sorrow, its joys and delights. We give thanks for the dear gift of death which is so much a part of life that the one is unimaginable without the other. Together they form the deep mystery of existence into which we are born.

Notes

CHAPTER 1

1. Arthur S. Peake, *A Commentary on the Bible* (London: Thomas Nelson and Sons, 1919), 136.
2. Lewis Thomas, *The Medusa and the Snail: More Notes of a Biology Watcher* (New York: Viking Press, 1974), 37–38.
3. Ibid., 39.

CHAPTER 2

1. Jane Gross, "McEnroe Overwhelms Connors," *New York Times*, 21 June 1984, B2.
2. Steven R. Weisman, "Reagan Calls for Drinking Age of 21," *New York Times*, 9 July 1984, C8.

CHAPTER 3

1. Robert Haven Schauffler, *Beethoven: The Man Who Freed Music* (New York: Tudor Publishing, 1947), 50.
2. Hannah Tillich, *From Time to Time* (New York: Stein and Day, 1973), 189–90.
3. Ibid., 104–5.
4. Roy D. Phillips, "Preaching as a Sacramental Event," in *Transforming Words: Six Essays on Preaching,* ed. William F. Schulz (Boston: Skinner House, 1984), 15ff.
5. William Butler Yeats, "The Circus Animals' Desertion," in *The Poems: A New Edition,* ed. Richard J. Finneran (New York: Macmillan, 1983), 346.

CHAPTER 4

1. William Shakespeare, *Julius Caesar,* 4.3.96–99.
2. Elisabeth Kübler-Ross, "Life, Death, and the Dying Patient," interview given at the University of Washington School of Medicine, 1982.

CHAPTER 5

1. Richard Swinburne, *The Concept of Miracle* (London: Macmillan, 1970), 11.
2. Ibid.
3. Isaiah Berlin, *Personal Impressions* (New York: Viking Press, 1980), 150–51.
4. Ibid., 61.
5. Jeffrey Bernhard, "Probing the Chemistry of Life," *Harvard Magazine* (September–October 1980): 23.

6. R. F. Holland, "The Miraculous," *American Philosophical Quarterly* 2 (1965):43–51.

7. John Noble Wilford, "Theory Ties Exodus Flood to Tidal Wave," *New York Times*, 4 May 1981.

8. W. H. Auden, "For the Time Being: A Christmas Oratorio," in *The Collected Poetry of W. H. Auden*, ed. Edward Mendelson (New York: Random House, 1976), 412.

CHAPTER 6

1. Frank DeFord, *Alex: The Life of a Child* (New York: Signet Books, 1983), 88.

2. William Shakespeare, *Hamlet*, 1.5.166–67.

3. James P. Markham, "Elie Wiesel Gets Nobel for Peace as 'Messenger,' " *New York Times*, 15 October 1986, A1, A10.

CHAPTER 7

1. Ivan Sergeyevich Turgenev, *Dream Tales and Prose Poems;* quoted in Victor Gollancz, *Man and God* (Boston: Houghton Mifflin, 1951), 51–52.

CHAPTER 8

1. Paul Tillich, *The Shaking of the Foundations* (New York: Charles Scribner's Sons, 1948), 165.

2. Wallace Stevens, "The Well-Dressed Man with a Beard," in *The Collected Poems of Wallace Stevens* (New York: Alfred A. Knopf, 1954), 247.

CHAPTER 10

1. *The Economist,* 16 October 1982, 29–30.
2. Lewis Thomas, *The Youngest Science: Notes of a Medicine Watcher* (New York: Viking Press, 1983), 29–30.

CHAPTER 11

1. Joachim Prinz, *Popes from the Ghetto: A View of Medieval Christendom* (New York: Horizon Press, 1966), 74.
2. Ibid.
3. Walt Whitman, "I Loafe and Invite My Soul," from "Leaves of Grass" in *The Poetry and Prose of Walt Whitman,* ed. Louis Untermeyer (New York: Simon and Schuster, 1949), 95.

CHAPTER 12

1. Paul Davies, *Other Worlds* (New York: Simon and Schuster, 1980), 183.
2. Ibid., 107.
3. Fritjof Capra, *The Tao of Physics* (Berkeley, Calif.: Shambhala, 1976), 56.
4. Ibid.
5. Pearl S. Buck, *The Child Who Never Grew* (New York: John Day, 1950), 31.
6. Robert Massie and Suzanne Massie, *Journey* (New York: Alfred A. Knopf, 1975).

CHAPTER 13

1. Joshua Loth Liebman, *Peace of Mind* (New

York: Simon and Schuster, 1946); Fulton J. Sheen, *Peace of Soul* (New York: Doubleday, 1954).

2. Augustus Y. Napier with Carl A. Whitaker, *The Family Crucible* (New York: Harper and Row, 1978), 191–92.

3. James Luther Adams, *On Being Human Religiously* (Boston: Beacon Press, 1976), 146.

4. Ibid.

CHAPTER 14

1. Reinhold Niebuhr, *The Nature and Destiny of Man* (New York: Charles Scribner's Sons, 1941), 2:22.

2. Joella Vreeland, "The Seeds of Violence," *Unitarian Universalist Women's Federation Journal* 2, no. 2 (15 May 1984).

3. Ibid.

4. Ibid.

5. Del Martin, *Battered Wives* (San Francisco: Glide Publications, 1976), 53.

6. See Fred Ferretti, "From Ashes of Tragedy, Self-Help Groups," *New York Times*, 4 June 1984.

7. Susan Griffin, *Pornography and Silence: Culture's Revolt against Nature* (New York: Harper and Row, 1981), 160.

CHAPTER 16

1. Leo Baeck, *The Pharisees and Other Essays* (New York: Schocken Books, 1947), 34.

2. Ibid., 34–35.

3. James Luther Adams, *The Prophethood of All Believers*, ed. George K. Beach (Boston: Beacon Press, 1986), 87.

4. Tom Morganthau et al., "Gay America in Transition," *Newsweek*, 8 August 1983, 33.

5. William Shakespeare, *Julius Caesar*, 1.2.140–41.

6. J. Robert Oppenheimer, *Science and the Common Understanding* (New York: Simon and Schuster, 1953), 40.

CHAPTER 17

1. Richard Quebedeaux, *The Worldly Evangelicals* (New York: Harper and Row, 1978), xi.

2. Ibid., 3–4.

3. Paul Tillich, quoted in Theodosius Dobzhanksy, "Evolution: Implications for Religion," *The Christian Century* (19 July 1967), 941.

CHAPTER 18

1. Robert Jastrow, *God and the Astronomers* (New York: W. W. Norton, 1978), 116.

2. Tom F. Driver, *Patterns of Grace: Human Experience as Word of God* (San Francisco: Harper and Row, 1977).

3. J. Robert Oppenheimer, *Science and the Common Understanding* (New York: Simon and Schuster, 1953), 69.

4. Gerhad von Rad, *Old Testament Theology*, vol. 1: *The Theology of Israel's Historical Traditions* (New York: Harper and Row, 1962), 109.

5. Frederick Turner, *Beyond Geography: The Western Spirit against the Wilderness* (New York: Viking Press, 1980), 118.

6. Paul Tillich, "The Lost Dimension in Religion," *Saturday Evening Post*, 14 June 1958, 29ff.

7. Idem, *Dynamics of Faith* (New York: Harper and Brothers, 1957), 45.

8. Driver, *Patterns of Grace*, 121.

9. Quoted in David Flusser, *Jesus* (Hamburg: Rowohlt Taschenbuch, 1968), 146.

10. G. Peter Fleck, *The Mask of Religion* (Buffalo, N.Y.: Prometheus Books, 1980), 11–12.

11. Robert McAfee Brown "Starting Over: New Beginning Points for Theology," *The Christian Century*, 14 May 1980, 547.

12. Bradford Smith, *Dear Gift of Life: A Man's Encounter with Death*, Pendle Hill Pamphlet 142 (1965), 13.

13. Driver, *Patterns of Grace*, 122–23.

CHAPTER 19

1. George Steiner, *In Bluebeard's Castle* (New Haven: Yale University Press, 1971), 53–54.

2. Samuel Sandmel, *We Jews and Jesus* (New York: Oxford University Press, 1965), 145.

3. Lucy Davidowicz, *The War against the Jews, 1933–1945* (New York: Holt, Rinehart and Winston, 1975), 149. See also Susan Griffin, *Pornography and Silence: Culture's Revolt against Nature* (New York: Harper and Row, 1981), 191.

4. Fyodor Dostoyevsky, *The Brothers Karamazov*, trans. David Magarshack (Harmondsworth: Penguin, 1958), 691.

5. Michael Novak, *A Time to Build* (New York: Macmillan, 1967), 68.

CHAPTER 20

1. Dorothee Sölle, *Lijden* (Baarn: Uitgeverij Bosch & Keuning, 1973), 70. My translation.

CHAPTER 21

1. Robert McAfee Brown, "Starting Over: New Beginning Points for Theology," *The Christian Century*, 14 May 1980, 547.
2. Archibald MacLeish, *J.B.: A Play in Verse* (Boston: Houghton Mifflin, 1958), 11.
3. Jacob J. Petuchowski, "Justice and Mercy in Judaism," lecture delivered to the Catholic Academy, Stuttgart-Hohenheim, 29 June 1979 (Rundbrief 31, 1979, no. 117/120). My translation.
4. Emmanuel Levinas, *Het Menselijk Gelaat* (Basisboeken/Ambo/Bilthoven, 1969), 53. My translation.
5. Ralph Wood, "John Updike's Rabbit Saga," *The Christian Century*, 20 January 1982, 51.
6. Thomas à Kempis, *Of the Imitation of Christ* (London: Oxford University Press, 1900), 3.17.131.
7. Harold S. Kushner, *When Bad Things Happen to Good People* (New York: Schocken Books, 1981), 85.

CHAPTER 22

1. C. D. B. Bryan, "A Lesson in Tragedy," *New York Times Magazine*, 23 February 1986, 32–37.

CHAPTER 23

1. Russell Baker, *Growing Up* (New York: New American Library, 1983), 38.
2. Bradford Smith, *Dear Gift of Life: A Man's Encounter with Death*, Pendle Hill Pamphlet 142 (1965), 35.
3. Dylan Thomas, *A Child's Christmas in Wales* (New York: New Directions, 1954), 31.

CHAPTER 24

1. P. N. van Eyck, *De Tuinman en de Dood*. My translation.

2. Henry David Thoreau, in *The Little, Brown Book of Anecdotes*, ed. Clifton Fadiman (Boston: Little, Brown, 1985), 543.

3. Bradford Smith, *Dear Gift of Life: A Man's Encounter with Death*, Pendle Hill Pamphlet 142 (1965), 15.

4. Dylan Thomas, "Do Not Go Gentle into That Good Night," in *The Poems*, ed. Daniel Jones (London: J. M. Dent and Sons, 1971), 207–8.

5. Smith, *Dear Gift of Life*, 9.

6. Walt Whitman, "Assurances," in *The Poetry and Prose of Walt Whitman*, ed. Louis Untermeyer (New York: Simon and Schuster, 1949), 406.

7. Ibid., "When Lilacs Last in the Dooryard Bloom'd," 323.

Index